The Moral Imagination and Public Life

CHATHAM HOUSE STUDIES IN POLITICAL THINKING
SERIES EDITOR: George J. Graham, Jr.
Vanderbilt University

THE MORAL IMAGINATION AND PUBLIC LIFE

Raising the Ethical Question

Thomas E. McCollough
Duke University

CHATHAM HOUSE PUBLISHERS, INC.
Chatham, New Jersey

THE MORAL IMAGINATION AND PUBLIC LIFE:
RAISING THE ETHICAL QUESTION

Chatham House Publishers, Inc.
Box One, Chatham, New Jersey 07928

Publisher: Edward Artinian
Cover design: Antler & Baldwin Design Group, Inc.
Production supervisor: Chris Kelaher
Composition: Bang, Motley, Olufsen
Printing and binding: BookCrafters

Library of Congress Cataloging-in-Publication Data

McCollough, Thomas E., 1926–
   The moral imagination and public life: raising the ethical
question / Thomas E. McCollough.
      p.   cm. — (Chatham House studies in political thinking)
   Includes bibliographical references and index.
   ISBN 0-934540-85-3
      1. Political ethics. 2. Policy sciences—Moral and ethical
aspects. I. Title. II. Series.
JA79.M36—1991
172—dc20   91-6821
                                                              CIP

Manufactured in the United States of America
            10 9 8 7 6 5 4 3 2 1

For Mary Lee

CONTENTS

ACKNOWLEDGMENTS

MORE than anything else, it has been the questions of students that have impelled me to press my exploration of the moral perspective on society and public life. Community has taken on deeper meaning as people have contributed in various ways to the development of this project.

Valued readers at earlier stages include Michael Gillespie, Gil Hedley, Betsy Jadlos, Anne Knowles, Tim Koch, Bruce Lawrence, Sy Mauskopf, Tim Patterson, Jim Price, Joe Sinsheimer, Shirley Strobel, and Ruel Tyson, many of whose remarks came to fruition. In conversations over the years James David Barber has been a frequent source of insights.

Six people were of invaluable help at critical points: Fred Bonner, whose moral support and Laptop Toshiba (courtesy of The Discovery Channel) triggered a quantum leap in technical efficiency and productivity; Bill Poteat, whose lunchtime conversations provided frequent clarification of ideas pivotal for my project; Larry Malley, who gave me generous editorial counsel and an introduction to Edward Artinian; Wanda Camp, whose staff assistance was a model of competence and grace; and Jodi-Beth McCain and Dean Miner, who as senior undergraduates helped stimulate and enliven the final stages of writing.

All along, there has been one without peer, Mary Lee Rankin McCollough, to whom I dedicate this book.

PREFACE

ETHICS as a discipline has an academic history. For the teacher of ethics, the shared enterprise of dialogue and discussion with colleagues and students is vital to the way in which ethical theory is conceived, as well as practiced. Early in my classroom experience I came to see the need for developing an interdisciplinary approach to political ethics, which at that time was largely confined to philosophy. A year at the London School of Economics in 1967–68, which was made possible by a Crossdisciplinary Fellowship from the Society for Religion in Higher Education, enabled me to work in the social sciences with a view to developing a political ethic that would be coherent, realistic, and constructive. Since then, I have come to appreciate increasingly the role of moral imagination in public life.

In thinking about the way we make moral decisions, it is easy to overlook the part that moral imagination plays. Moral imagination is energized and expanded as we remember and reflect on those experiences in which we empathize with others and try to find ways to meet their needs and take action on their behalf. When such moments are shared by a group, they may become part of a community's moral heritage. It was so with students who joined in a vigil in 1968.

The spring of 1968 will remain in the memory of many Americans as long as they live. Martin Luther King, Jr., was assassinated, then Robert Kennedy. Those two deaths symbolized the trauma and tragedy of Vietnam abroad and the civil rights struggle at home. For Americans living abroad at the time, it was painful, yet somehow not quite real.

My family and I were in England for the year. Early that spring, I received a letter from a student who had been in my ethics class the previous spring. She said she was writing from the quad in front of the university chapel, where she was sitting in silence, along with 1500 other students and a few faculty members. They were calling on the university to correct racially based inequities in the pay and treatment of its employees.

For four days and nights that week in April 1968, a large group of students and a number of faculty sat on the grassy quadrangle in the center of the university, with the declared intention to stay there until their demands for racial justice were met by the university's board of trustees. The vigil concluded five days later when, after extended negotiation, the distinguished and elderly chairman of the board linked arms with the students and stood with them in the misting rain to sing "We Shall Overcome." Though it was not long before the chairman of the board of trustees and the president of the university were gone, the university yielded to the pressure of the vigil, recognizing the validity of the demands.

The vigil has become a moral symbol in the life of the university and in the life of those who participated in it. To celebrate the twentieth anniversary of the vigil, the "vigilites" gathered for a long weekend of recollection and introspection in September 1988, which they titled "The Duke Vigil: Twenty Years Later." Some 150 members from the classes of 1967 to 1971 returned to campus to assess how faithful the participants had been to the values of the vigil after twenty years. They were also interested in talking with students about what the university should be doing to further the cause of justice. One of them said, "People who are coming here would not go to typical class reunions. Those are too vacuous. These folks have a hunger for significance" (*The Duke Chronicle,* 26 September 1988, p. 1).

The vigilites talked to sociology classes and in a ten-person panel on Saturday morning reflected on the vigil's continuing significance in their lives. Several admitted to fears about coming back, apprehension at analyzing their lives in the light of the vigil. But they found amid the diversity of their present lives a bond that had remained vital. One said, "We were all touched by a kind of fire during the vigil. We've gone on circuitous tracks but have maintained that spark." Those "circuitous tracks" were evident in the careers represented: a Zen Buddhist, two mayors, a banker from the South Bronx, Peace Corps volunteers, inner-city schoolteachers, writers, and college professors. Later, one participant, a clinical psychologist, told me that he was troubled by his lack of political activity but that he judges his life by what he experienced in the vigil.

During the reunion, one said, "I couldn't even remember the four demands of the vigil. Once I did get through them, I couldn't remember the results, which made me realize that what was really important was the process and the people" (ibid.).

The meaning of the vigil cannot be assessed on a statistical basis. It is found in the commitments played out in the lives of those for whom it remains a transforming moral experience. It has also become a part of the history of the university.* At the turn of the century, Professor John Spencer Bassett of Trinity College (later to become Duke University) was widely attacked for his statement that Robert E. Lee and Booker T. Washington were the two greatest men in the South. When Bassett offered to resign, he was asked by Trinity's president and trustees to remain on the faculty. President Theodore Roosevelt in a Durham speech commended the college, and it was widely recognized for making a courageous stand in protection of free speech. A former faculty member, later a member of the university's board of trustees, who participated in the vigil has observed that along with the "Bassett affair," the vigil has exercised a continuing influence on the board of trustees. Actions over the past several years—the university's decision to divest itself of stock in South Africa, a mandate to hire black faculty in every department in the university, and ventures in cooperation with the student homeless project—are moments in the history of the university that have some moral continuity with the Bassett affair and the vigil. This event and its resonance in the lives of the participants and the university provide a starting point for our reflection on the moral relation of the citizen to public life.

---

* A firsthand account is given by then-President Douglas M. Knight in his *Street of Dreams: The Nature and Legacy of the* 1960s (Durham: Duke University Press, 1989), 118–24.

And [the Lord] answered and said to me . . .

"For just as you have not forgotten the people who now are, and those who have passed away, so I remember those who are to come."

— 2 Baruch 23:3

1

PUBLIC POLICY AND THE
ETHICAL QUESTION

THE WORLD WAS STUNNED by the democratic eruptions that took place across Eastern Europe as the decade of the eighties was coming to a close. As people under communist rule spontaneously rose up in massive protest, their authoritarian governments crumbled. Citizens in long-established democratic countries rejoiced with them in their new freedom. In the days following, however, reactions in the West began to include some sobering questions. How could countries without a tradition of self-government and democratic institutions become viable democracies, especially when most of them lacked economic security and stability?

There were those in Western countries who were ready to help. Experienced politicians, political scientists, economists, and others served as consultants, including some political media experts who were ready to advise political candidates on how to run and win by exploiting the opportunities of the media. Perhaps it was the prospect of negative campaigning in the new democracies that began to prompt a different question: How about American democracy? A recent expensive, glitzy, and vacuous presidential campaign; voter apathy; and the massive denial of critical social and economic problems by politicians and voters alike led some to wonder, occasionally out loud, When will there be a democratic uprising in the United States of America?

Americans disheartened at the national failure to deal imaginatively and effectively with the issues confronting us have begun to take hope in the possibilities unleashed by the democratic revolutions in Europe. There are signs of hope also in many grass-roots citizen movements in this country. Collective action will be required in order to solve the problems of environmental pollution, health care, unemployment, poverty, and the homeless. Who will initiate this action? How will these decisions be made? Will they be just, and will they preserve and enhance the common good? What is the responsibility of the citizen in democratic decision making? We begin with a critical examination of some current ways of thinking about political life and public ethics in order to frame the central problem to which this book is addressed.

Public Policy and Political Life

Whereas classical political philosophy was concerned with the normative questions of the nature of man, the good life, and the good society, political scientists have tended to limit their study to a description of institutions and their constitutional justification. Modern behavioral political science has focused primarily on governmental processes and behaviors, what *is*, rather than what *ought* to be. Almost two decades ago, a political scientist noted that "the focus of political science is shifting to *public policy—to the description and explanation of the causes and consequences of government activity*."[1] The study of public policy includes an evaluation of the societal impact of public policies. The rapid growth of "policy studies" in the past two decades reflects the need to acquire knowledge about society and the process of policy making in order to improve the quality of public policy. The interest in public policy analysis can be traced in part to the attempt of social scientists to apply scientific methods to policy analysis; in part, no doubt, to the fascination of academics with political power and the possibility of access to it afforded by their work; but, finally, in large part to the felt need to bring some rational order and planning to policy making.

Public policy has been defined as a course of action chosen by government that affects large numbers of people.[2] An even broader definition includes "whatever governments choose to do or not to do." Public policy has to do with the clarification of objectives. In a widely quoted definition, David Easton says that policy is "the authoritative allocation of values for the whole society."[3] The fact that policy decisions are value choices may seem obvious enough to the ordinary person, but it has posed major problems for the policy scientist, who typically has assumed a value-neutral posture. Harold Lasswell could write in the late 1960s that it was the "obviously overt value content of public policy questions" that accounted for the fact that the field of public policy had been "relatively untouched by rigorous scientific investigation."[4]

The growth of public policy "sciences" (along with a constantly growing number of moral issues such as governmental corruption, corporate fraud, poverty and unemployment, pollution of the environment) has brought the value question to the fore. The selection of social problems for analysis and public choice, the evaluation of the impact of policies, recommendations of policy priorities, all involve value judgments and choices. The ethical question is whether these judgments are made explicit and are open to critical examination, public debate, and democratic choice.

While citizens may want policy to be arrived at by democratic means, they also want it to be informed and effective. Political scientists such as Charles Lindblom make much of the conflict between *intelligence* (information and critical analysis) and *democracy* (conceived as the "play of power" or "popular control").[5] Intelligence becomes the function of the policy analyst, in practice the policy scientist or expert. Two models of policy analysis, rational-comprehensive and incremental, have figured significantly in the literature of public policy studies. The two models of policy analysis describe quite different approaches to policy making.[6] The *rational-comprehensive* model is conspicuous in the literature of economics, political science, business, and engineering. This approach calls for the policy maker to identify the problem; to survey citizen preferences, giving them relative weights; to canvass all possible solutions and their consequences; and to select the most efficient policy option. Critics point out serious obstacles to this scientific ideal of policy analysis. The model is feasible only if the problem is simple, if there is a single objective, and if there are few political constraints. Policy makers do not have the information, the time, the knowledge, or the intellectual capacity to make comprehensive, rational, scientific decisions.

Advocates of the *incremental* model take a "strategic" approach to policy making, which is more pragmatic and conservative. This model relies on the uncoordinated working of the market and the pluralism of the political process. In this view, the policy maker, typically an administrator, proceeds by trial and error, taking a modest step that is politically expedient. Proponents of this approach do not reject the scientific ideal but see it as both unattainable and nonpolitical. Analysis is not comprehensive and disinterested; as employed in the political process, it is partisan analysis.

The advocates of the rational-comprehensive model favor centralized administration and planning; incrementalists want to keep authority diffused. But both assume a broad value consensus or ideological framework that in America may be characterized as "pluralist democracy" and "corporate enterprise."[7] This ideological assumption limits the specific issues that can be raised as matters for public policy making, how the issues will be viewed, and the range of options open to decision makers. Although Lindblom earlier saw this ideology of corporate capitalism as enabling democratic policy making to function efficiently, he later took a more critical view. In a comparative analysis of economic efficiency and democratic freedom in capitalistic and socialist societies, he concluded: "It is difficult to see how the corporation fits into democratic theory. Indeed, it does not fit."[8] It is hard to conceive of a more fundamental challenge to incrementalism than the one posed here by Lindblom, who himself first characterized the model.

Limitations of This Approach

When politics is narrowed to policy making, public policy takes on the semblance of a rational decision by a governmental mind. The shift from democratic decision making to policy making narrows the focus to a leadership elite of policy analysts and policy makers responsible for the determination of policy. This managerial approach of democratic elitism conceives of politics as governmental procedures rather than deliberative action by the civil community. The question then becomes that of the best techniques available for analyzing policy issues from a rational, comprehensive perspective.

The rational-comprehensive model of "synoptic rationality," and typically the incremental model as well, presuppose a view of the policy sciences characterized by its critics as scientism. In this view, fact is sharply distinguished from value. Fact is taken to be empirically verifiable; value is held to be emotive only, the statement of individual preference, taste, or opinion. *Scientism* is the attempted application of the practice and theory of the natural sciences to social and political life. Although it is widely discredited by natural scientists and philosophers, it retains its hold as an ideal by many social scientists and, among them, policy analysts. The scientific ideal of rational policy making carries with it the idea that policy experts are essential to the process. The expert represents intelligence, in contrast to the supposed irrationality of democratic decision making.[9] Scientism makes reason the function of the expert, whose purportedly value-free knowledge deflects the question of political interest and privilege and preserves the status quo.

Democratic elitism reserves policy making for the government both because of the presumption that rational decision making requires scientific policy analysis and because in this view participatory democracy involves conflicting and "irrational" values. In this view, political discourse is irrational and detrimental to the policy-making process. Besides, insofar as the ideal of democracy is concerned, "power is equally distributed among millions of citizens with the consequence that no single citizen enjoys more than a tiny, nearly useless share."[10]

The citizen is then remote from the policy making process, impotent and alienated. Small wonder that the ordinary American citizen is found by pollsters to be apathetic.

The Problem Stated

The problem to which this book is addressed may now be stated in the following way: The view of political life as a policy-making process, with decisions made by a democratic elite employing policy analysts (experts), has two fateful consequences. First, public discussion of the ethical issues is devalued and is seen as extraneous to policy making. Ethics enters into the process only as an arbitrary function of the individual decision maker. Second, the citizen is rendered remote, powerless, alienated, apathetic, and hopeless.

The problem is compounded by the conventional view of ethics that conceives the relation of ethics to public policy as a matter of bringing to bear ethical principles in the analysis of policy issues. These principles are typically derived from classical philosophical ethics, notably the traditions

of Kantian and utilitarian ethics. Since philosophical reasoning is not applied in the process of policy making, it is typically the preoccupation of
professional ethicists, examining policy outcomes in retrospect.

Is it possible to reconceive democratic polity and ethics so as to disclose an integral and moral relation between the ethically concerned citizen and political decision making?

The Quest for a Public Ethic

Perhaps the top-down view of politics as policy making just sketched could
be moderated by an ethical perspective. Could ethical principles be applied
to policy making in order to achieve more humane and productive outcomes? In view of the regnant scientism, it would seem to be unlikely. A
policy science that divides fact and value, and relegates values to the private sphere of individual preference, is not likely to be open to ethical
analysis. Nor is there any way to ensure that the policy-making elite will
choose to bring ethical principles to bear on their decision making. Beyond that, ethics itself has traditionally reflected a rationalistic bias similar
to that found in policy scientists.

The attempt to apply classical ethical principles to public policy analysis confronts several obstacles. For one, because ethical principles are general and abstract, they are remote from the concrete situation and the
specific considerations entailed in reaching an appropriate decision. But,
more telling yet, in actual practice we seldom make decisions on the basis
of conscious and comprehensive reflection on ethical principles as such. In
order to show why this is so and to indicate an alternative view of ethics, it
is necessary to distinguish between ethics and morality.

The word ethics comes from the Greek word *ethos,* meaning custom,
usage, or character. "Morality" and "ethics" are often used interchange-
ably. Though they have a common root meaning in the Greek *ethos* and
the Latin *mores,* they have come to signify different aspects of experience.
It is important to keep these distinctions in mind when considering the relation of ethics and public policy.

Morality refers to commonly accepted rules of conduct, patterns of
behavior approved by a social group, values and standards shared by the

group. It consists of beliefs about what is good and right held by a community with a shared history. *Ethics* is the critical analysis of morality. It is reflection on morality with the purpose of analysis, criticism, interpretation, and justification of the rules, roles, and relations of a society.[11] Ethics is concerned with the meaning of moral terms, the conditions in which moral decision making takes place, and the justification of the principles brought to bear in resolving conflicts of value and of moral rules.

A number of contemporary ethicists characterize the moral point of view as that in which "one is doing things on principle, one is willing to universalize one's principles, and in doing so one considers the good of everyone alike."[12] This textbook definition of ethics, or "the moral point of view," is open to some of the same criticisms that are aimed at the policy sciences.

The aim of the major Western ethicists has been to discern and state rational principles on which all persons of goodwill and sound reason could agree. This has led ethicists to search for foundational principles that would transcend the relative historical particularities of the ethicist's situation and constitute unchanging norms of universal validity. Inevitably and necessarily, these principles, whether of Immanuel Kant's categorical imperative or Jeremy Bentham's greatest happiness principle, have been so abstract as to require a great deal of interpretation and discretionary judgment on the part of the decision maker. The ongoing history of philosophical ethics testifies to the ambiguities and limitations of these principles. Both ethics and policy analysis need to be reconceived in terms of a more realistic understanding of human reason and a more democratic view of decision making.

Reasoning about moral choice can be viewed from two quite different perspectives: as reasoning about ethical principles in the light of the traditions of philosophical ethics (e.g., Kantian or utilitarian), with a view to applying them to a moral issue; or as reasoning about what is to be done in a concrete situation, in the light of who one is and what one is called on to do. The first is appropriate when a moral issue is analyzed by philosophers or theologians, the second has to do with the way we make ethical decisions as moral agents in a decision-making situation. Consider the way one would go about making an ethical decision in a real-life ("boiler room") situation, in contrast to textbook ethics.

Two Test Cases

Imagine yourself as the student leader of a sit-in. President and trustees have dragged their feet in responding to demands, and people on the quad have lost patience and are getting restless. There is talk about doing something that will put more pressure on the administration. Tempers rise, and a murmur turns into the chant "Burn it down!" Suddenly the crowd surges toward the administration building. You manage to work your way to the front of the crowd just as it reaches the main door of the building. You are able to get the crowd to stop for a moment. What will you say? As student leader of the sit-in, you know that you have a just cause and that success depends on group solidarity in the pursuit of that cause. To try to turn the group back now may be to lose its support; to allow it to press into the building may be to pave the way for a dramatic victory or may result in property damage, arrests, and possibly the discrediting of what has been done so far. What is your decision as to the right course of action, and how will you appeal to the group?

Or imagine yourself in the place of the president of the university. How will you respond to the demands of those sitting-in on the quad? What will you say to the press? What course of action will you recommend to the board of trustees? You will probably not turn to your old college textbook from the philosophy course in ethics, nor will you likely consult a professor of ethics. You will not find much help in the university charter, nor even in your own presidential addresses describing the ideals and goals of the institution. The situation is perplexing precisely because it is novel and without precedent in your own experience. What should you do? As president, you are mindful of the implications of this event for the university, its public image, its constituencies. You know that university employees are underpaid, but you know also that an increase in compensation will severely tax an already strained budget. You yourself are in sympathy with the aim of the demonstrators, but if you accede to their demands, you can expect to be criticized for "giving in to a bunch of campus radicals."

In each situation, you want to do the right thing. How do you arrive at an intelligent, principled decision with personal integrity? Would you take a few minutes out in order to refresh your mind on the principles of metaphysics? Reread your Kant and Bentham? Not likely, and not simply

for lack of time. Textbook ethics is far removed from boiler-room decision making. In the boiler room itself, how do you reach solid ground in
ethical reflection? Actually, we have to consider here two different but related questions: How does one go about making an ethical decision in a
particular situation? And how does one justify that decision, whether personal or public, to others?

Are personal and public decisions essentially different? The first may
seem to be a function of subjective feeling, intuition, and conscience, of
character and internalized values; the second, a matter of impersonal reason, with appeal to objective principles. But public decision making discloses some of the features of individual decision making. It reflects the
character and personal and community history of the persons making the
decisions. The way in which ethical principles are made explicit and are
accredited, the analysis and justification of decision making, is similar for a
private person and for public decision makers. This calls for a way of understanding ethics significantly different from that of textbook ethics.

Ethics as the Critical Analysis of Morality

In contrast to ethicists who characterize the moral point of view as that in
which one does things on principle, universalizes one's principles, and
considers the good of everyone alike,[13] others take a different approach,
which has been characterized as "visional ethics."[14] Instead of stressing the
importance of the universalizability of principles, these ethicists are more
concerned with the concrete relationships and way of life of moral subjects. For the first group, ethics is primarily a matter of principled reasoning about moral choices. For the second, ethics has more to do with
character, virtue, vision, and the stories of the communities that shape the
moral life.

In an influential essay, the philosopher-novelist Iris Murdoch contended that the legacy of the Enlightenment, Romanticism, and the Liberal tradition has been "far too shallow and flimsy an idea of human personality."[15] As found in philosophical ethics, the modern person is rational,
totally free, and totally responsible for all his or her acts. He or she is pictured as naked will; his or her fundamental virtue is sincerity. In this ac-

count, ethics is reduced to choice. Against the abstract, rationalistic rendering of ethics, advocates of visional ethics stress the importance of narrative, imagination, character, responsibility, relationships, and forms of life or ways of being in the world, the ethics of character in community.

The two perspectives in ethics are not mutually exclusive. Both are needed in order to complement each other. Visional ethics corresponds more closely with morality, principled reasoning with ethics. The two approaches constitute two different views of the moral agent as *person-in-community* and as *individual-in-society*. As person-in-community, one shares the morality of a community with a common history, shared values, tradition, and cultural ethos. As an individual in a pluralistic society, one seeks to arrive at universal ethical principles. Ethical decision is both *individual,* in that one is responsible for one's own rational analysis and attempt to arrive at universally valid principles, and *personal,* in that one speaks out of one's own history and group morality. What one "knows" is personal knowledge, a function of one's own participation in community. If one seeks universal validity, it is on the basis of tacit assumptions shared in varying degree with other selves in relation to whom one seeks to validate truth claims.

It is appropriate to conceive of ethics as disciplined reflection on *usages,*[16] that is, morally authoritative ways of thinking about ourselves and our common life. Ethical reflection consists, then, not of analysis and application of principles derived from historical texts, but of critical analysis of what we say, what we do, what we are. It can be aptly described in words that Wayne Booth used to define rhetoric: "the art of discovering warrantable beliefs and improving those beliefs in a shared discourse."[17] Ethics in this view is not the private enterprise of philosopher, theologian, or public policy maker but a venture in which persons test their beliefs in conversation with others. In order to sharpen moral perception and to make ethical judgment, one examines our usages, the way we talk about social practices, value traditions, institutional rituals, admired persons. These usages are the music (and static) of our daily lives. Public ethics is an ongoing conversation about how to discern and compose the lyrics to this music.

Morality, then, is to be understood as a way of life, common and exemplary usages, embedded in a whole network of practices, beliefs, attitudes, a "way of being in the world," a "lifeworld" that phenomenologists have sought to describe. Moral judgments are not simply "emotive," expressions of how people feel, but cognitive claims about how things are, that is, moral knowledge. In this regard, moral judgments are similar to scientific judgments. Both represent our considered beliefs about reality and are subject to critical testing in experience and by others.

The ground of ethical appeal is not abstract rational principles but a worthy moral life. This may not be definable in a way that will muster universal consent, but it can be indicated in terms such as "a life well lived," a "flourishing life," a life that has "achieved well-being," "a long and happy life."[18]

Our appeal, then, is not to principles or rules or "oughts," but to a way of life that we know, respect, admire, would like to emulate and share. Moral authority resides in what we know to be a way of life commended by the moral community to which we belong. Notice that this view of morality is not moralistic. That is, it does not demand compliance with a code of conduct or set of moral rules or even rational ethical principles from a morally superior perspective. It does not claim the privileged position of an ethical judge external to the life of the person whose behavior is under scrutiny. Instead, it asks, Given the opportunity to reflect on this act or practice or belief, how does it accord with your view of the well-lived life? Is it consonant with your aspirations and vision of well-being? Would it contribute to or hinder the relations with others that make for a fully realized life? Is it something you admire in others? Would you commend it to those you love and respect the most? Is it something you will value and appreciate a decade from now; at the end of your life? Does it advance you toward the self you want finally to be? But just what is the *self*?

The Ethical Self

The category of ethical choice tends to be taken for granted in ethical analyses of public policy. Unless there is a "knot in the thread," however, the moral fabric of personality and of society itself will unravel. The metaphor of the knot in the thread is that of Søren Kierkegaard, for whom the category of ethical choice is the key to the mystery of the human personality. Here Kierkegaard remains the most perceptive teacher, laying bare the dynamics of the ethical self in a way unsurpassed by later psychologists and ethicists. We do well to recall his account of the way in which one becomes a self, lest in the examination of public life we forget ourselves.

Kierkegaard delineates three modes of existence: the aesthetic, the ethical, and the religious.[19] He speaks of them as "stages upon life's way," though they are not strictly sequential nor developmental stages through which everyone passes. They are spheres of existence, or "ways of being-in-the-world," as phenomenologists say. The ethical and religious stages are essentially related for Kierkegaard. One who takes his duty seriously will find a clue to the Eternal. For our purposes, it is the analysis of the aesthetic and the ethical modes that is important for social ethics.

Aesthetic individuals are uncommitted because they have not given birth to themselves. They have not actualized their subjectivity. Today, "subjectivity" tends to be a pejorative word, referring to that which is arbitrary and, because opposed to the "reality" of objectivity, tenuous and unreal. But, for Kierkegaard, subjectivity is the mode in which the self exists as *subject of his or her own life*. "Subjectivity is truth" because as one assumes responsibility for moral choice, one begins to realize the truth of one's existence as a self. In the aesthetic mode, one is an observer, detached and neutral. In the ethical mode, one is a participant, responsible and committed. In the aesthetic mode, the environment is the determinant of feeling and direction and "the center is the circumference," so there is no genuine selfhood. But in the ethical mode, the self is subject, the agent who determines the meaning and direction of his or her life; as such, "the self is the center." One becomes a centered self (not "self-centered") in the moment of ethical decision.

The process of becoming a self begins when one chooses to choose; more specifically, when one chooses the categories of good and evil. In moving from the aesthetic to the ethical stage, one chooses not simply a particular good but the good itself, in the sense of willing "the good." In choosing the good, one actualizes the self as subject of one's own life. For the ethical person, duty has the force of an eternal command which awakens the subject's sense of his or her own eternal validity as a self. Kierkegaard does not "spiritualize" the self; the ethical self is the whole person, the knowing, feeling, willing self. In one's totality as an existing historical being, one is constituted an integral self by recognizing an unconditional obligation, the ethical.

When we exercise ethical consciousness, we are open to the continual critical examination that characterizes scientific knowing. Not speculation but a questioning drive toward that which we hold most true and most important is the essence of ethical reflection. Such reflection is contextual in that we begin where we are, in a human community with bonds of shared values and common commitments, and in a concrete situation with a unique configuration of factors that bear significantly on the judgment and decision toward which we are groping. It is not bound by this immediate context but presses toward the absolute ground of ethical consciousness, ultimate concern, universal intent. In this sense moral knowledge is more certain than scientific, because it is unchanging, and more important, because of its unconditional imperative. Think only of the fundamental moral imperative, the Golden Rule: "Do unto others as you would have them do unto you." Variations of this rule appear in all the major world religions, testimony to its unchanging and unconditional nature. Has any scientific law stood the test of time as long as the Golden Rule?

Posing the Ethical Question

How might we formulate the ethical question in such a way as to ensure an essential moral relation between oneself as knower and actor and the public sphere? I propose a vantage point for ethical analysis in which we pose the ethical question as *What is my personal relation to what I know?* While this formulation may not seem appropriate for the collective enterprise of public ethics because it reflects the viewpoint of the single actor, it is the starting point for responsible analysis of public policy. It secures the vital connection between the self and the civil community. The ethical question impels members of the civil community to reason together about the good, right, and fitting on the basis of what we know and value in order to engage in responsible action.

What I know and value is grounded in the accumulated experience of the community. In formulating the ethical question in terms of my personal relation to what I know, the appeal is not to feeling, "pure reason," or intuition. It is to knowledge that is historical and social and personal, tacit as well as explicit. As Abraham Kaplan has said concerning a philosophy of politics, "it is a search for those inferential links by which each man can fasten together all he knows and loves and bind it to the fabric of his life among other men."[20] Certitude is found, to the degree that it is possible, in the interrelation of the whole complex of beliefs, ideals, values, loyalties, commitments, and knowledge that is the nexus between our self-identity and social ethos.

This approach is not intuitional but historical-contextual. An understanding of knowledge as essentially and inescapably historical in nature[21] will help preserve ethics from the illusions of idealism and rationalism, as well as the dangers of moralism. When we steadfastly refuse to detach values from their rootage in history and community, we can enter into moral discourse with our fellows, open to the possibility both of revising our own value judgments and of persuading others on the basis of reasoning together about values and principles. We can acknowledge both the relativity of values (i.e., their contextual relatedness) and the absolute dimension of ethical concern.

To state the ethical question as *What is my personal relation to what I know?* is to relate *knowledge* to its human, historical context and to assume *responsibility* for knowledge within that setting. So stated, the ethical question provides the knot in the thread, lacking which the whole social fabric unravels. The moral factor in the process is created by those who take responsibility for acknowledging it as binding on them—making them accountable to it and thus to others who also hold it.[22]

Ethical analysis of policy making is of potential value only insofar as it can be expected to affect the outcome in some way. Moral standards have binding force only on those who acknowledge them. It follows that they must be traced to those who articulate and uphold them, whether citizens, policy analysts, or policy makers. To raise the ethical question as *What is my personal relation to what I know?* is to inquire into my relation to the community in whose knowledge I participate. It leads me to press the moral question beyond What ought I to do in this situation? to What are my deepest intimations of what it is to live a well-lived life? What do I know about what it means to be human that would point me in the right direction here and now? What does my community keep alive as images of the flourishing life, and what do I know that enables me to envision my life in their light? How, then, does this bear on public ethics?

Public Ethics

Ethical analysis of social problems can be pursued on two levels. The first is that of specific policy issues in areas such as poverty, education, and civil liberties. The interests involved here are many, conflicting, and often difficult to reconcile or balance. Knowledge is limited, and the power to act decisively is restricted by inadequate resources and opposing interest groups. The issues can be publicly debated, however, and policies formulated and executed. The second level of ethical analysis is that of the cultural context, or ethos, of policy making. Here ethical analysis engages the question of the prevailing conception of knowledge, the dominant cultural values, and the institutional power structures that determine, though not absolutely, which social problems will be publicly defined as such and so become matters of policy choice. Sometimes a specific policy issue such as federal funding for the artificial heart will lead some to question the way in which societal institutions serve the best interests of citizens as, for example, in weighing the relative benefits of high-technology medicine for a few versus expanded preventive and primary health care for all.

The term *public ethics* has gained some currency over the past two decades, even as the social science discipline of *policy studies* has developed. While agreeing that public ethics must be interdisciplinary, some confine the term to the analysis and evaluation of specific issues whereas others use it in a much broader sense. Among those who take the broad view of public ethics, James Sellars has proposed public ethics as the study of national character or ethos. As the study of manners and morals, it would be the organizing discipline of American studies.[23] Of those who hold that public ethics should be confined to particular and pressing problems, Albert Jonsen and Lewis Butler have contended that public ethics needs to be distinguished from social ethics, which is too general to be of much use to policy makers. The tasks of public ethics in this view are "(1) articulation of relevant moral principles in the policy problem; (2) elucidation of proposed policy options in light of relevant moral principles; and (3) displaying ranked order of moral options for policy choice."[24]

Clearly, both broad and specific conceptions of public ethics are necessary. To attempt to separate them is to endanger the essential relation between morality and ethics. Specific policy issues raise the broader questions of cultural values and institutional arrangements that may have to be critically examined if the ethical question is pursued. Consideration of whether to grant federal funds for the development of the artificial heart should take into account competing values such as technological progress and free enterprise on the one hand and the values of the public health tradition (community, common good, equal access) on the other. The ethical question should be stated in such a way as to include morality and ethics: the springs of action in our deepest moral selves and the ethical principles by which our common life is to be regulated.

The ethical question can be defined in ways that range from the most general to the specific. To raise the ethical question, first, is to distinguish it from other kinds of questions, such as the political question or the religious question. On the most abstract level, it is a question of the good, the right, and the fitting. In public ethics it is, fundamentally, the question of the basic principles of democratic society, justice, and the common good, and, specifically, particular issues, such as injustice, corruption, pollution, genetic engineering. If it is to issue in the question of action, What are we to do? then the ethical question must be finally understood as *What is my personal relation to what I know?* Ethical policy making requires that citizens hold one another accountable for what they know and value. This calls into play both reason and moral imagination.

The Moral Imagination

The moral imagination may be understood as the capacity to empathize with others and to discern creative possibilities for ethical action. The moral imagination considers an issue in the light of the whole. The whole is not only the complex interrelated functional aspects of society, economic, political, social institutions. It is also the traditions, beliefs, values, ideals, and hopes of its members, who constitute a community with a stake in the good life and a hopeful future. The moral imagination broadens and deepens the context of decision making to include the less tangible but most meaningful feelings, aspirations, ideals, relationships. It encompasses the core values of personal identity, loyalties, obligations, promises, love, trust, and hope. Ethical judgment consists in making these values explicit and taking responsibility for judging their implications for action.

Americans are notoriously pragmatic and prone to be preoccupied with technique, the technological know-how of problem solving. Since we tend to set for ourselves only those problems that can be solved[25] whether in science or technology, the difficult, complex, interrelated social problems that are not amenable to technological solution fail to get sustained attention. In an instant culture in which the attention span is short and interruptions frequent and distracting, concentration on major questions is difficult. In view of the difficulty of attaining common understanding, the appeal of technique as the focus of agreement is great.

If what we know is reduced to technological knowledge, it will exclude that which gives it meaning and value and that which would enable human beings—political beings—to appropriate it in humanly meaningful ways. Human reason is exercised in technological, instrumental reasoning and, preeminently, in reasoning about ends, goals, values, standards, principles. Reason seeks understanding on the basis of faith that we *can* know, that knowledge is truly related to reality, that knowledge is good and that it ought to be used *aright* and for the *good*. The more bits and pieces of knowledge are fitted together in social and technical theory, the more necessary it is to relate them to the intangibles, the tacit values, human qualities of community.

The humanistic perspective must complement the behavioral approach to policy making with a wholistic, dramatic view of the individual as actor, responding and not simply reacting as a passive object.[26] The bias of behavioral models in the social sciences is to treat the act of an individual as the result of external forces, part of a process. Jacques Barzun stresses the limitations of a behavioral science that proceeds as in physical science by framing the scientific object by analysis and abstraction: "That man's manifestations of himself do not exist as separable parts is shown by the extreme difficulty of defining his powers, motives, virtues, and intellectual creations. None of the interesting things about man—love, poetry, humor, wit, despair, happiness—can be transfixed."[27] As the matrix of personhood and the context for the moral imagination, moral community includes the emotions and the creative imagination along with cognitive and social development.[28]

The understanding of a dramatic work of art, indeed, the method of the humanities, is to seek the meaning of the whole in the interconnections of the parts, beyond and not exclusively in its particulars.[29] The literal mind must inevitably misconstrue the significance of an event when it tries to understand it only in terms of what is obvious, explicit and determinate. The symbolic imagination grasps the meaning of the whole, including the life of emotions, of unspoken but deeply felt relationships, of aspirations, loyalties, and ideals—of what is intended and hoped for, as well as what is done. It involves the whole person, a whole way of life and a vision of life as a whole.[30]

Values require a broad context of meaning, to which technical reason is oblivious. The pervasive tendency to reduce the scope of reason by limiting knowledge to the technical excludes or ignores humanistic or moral knowledge. René Descartes, father of modern philosophy, stands as the classic representative of the conception of knowledge that has dominated Western thinking increasingly since the seventeenth century. The bedrock of certainty on which Descartes proposed to build philosophy was the proposition "I think, therefore I am." Thinking was given priority over the thinker. It followed that thought was given priority over thinking, then knowledge over thought, and finally the most objective and technical knowledge over knowledge, so that the most real is the most remote and detached from my being as existential thinker. "If it should turn out to be true that knowledge (in the modern sense of know-how) and thought have parted company for good," declares Hannah Arendt, "then we would indeed become the helpless slaves, not so much of our machines as of our know-how, thoughtless creatures at the mercy of every gadget which is technically possible, no matter how murderous it is."[31]

Value and Community

The difficulty of raising the ethical question is traceable to two related conceptual commitments: *knowledge* understood as objective and impersonal, and *value* conceived as subjective and equated with self-interest. The ideal of knowledge as objective, impersonal, and wholly explicit renders the knower incidental and expendable. Inevitably the concrete, interior reality of the self is felt to be alien to the "real" world. The objectivist view of knowledge undermines the ground of valuation and erodes the sense of identity.

A moral perspective on value distinguishes it from individual preference and interest. An individual's interests are private, held and defined by the individual without necessary reference to anyone else. A basic tenet of liberalism as stated by John Stuart Mill is that individuals are best qualified to define their own interests. Interests represent preferences, a matter of individual taste. Values, however, are communal. They are public in that they are standards transcending individual taste, carrying a claim to be recognized by the community. They can be discussed, analyzed, ordered, justified in rational discourse.[32] A meaningful discussion about values presupposes a common lifeworld, a shared cultural context within which persons respect one another and care about ideas and values as determinants of their life together.

Without confidence in our common experience as a basis for value judgment, we shall lack any sense of purpose and direction as a society, which means we will be vulnerable by default to those forces that do have a momentum and direction of their own. Values may seem far less real than factual information, which can be quantified and aggregated. But when traced to their source and examined within the contexts of the communities holding them, values have a backing in social reality. When communal values, such as clean air, aesthetic surroundings, liberty, equality, and justice, are not acknowledged, we are prepared to say they *ought* to be. They are values that command the assent and service of the community as a whole. They constitute the common good. The common good is not a part of the calculations of the marketplace mentality, which provides no inner check on the motive of maximizing private interest. Moral constraint on aggrandizing self-interest is a function of the shared values, common loyalties, and acceptance of mutual obligations in the civic community. Only in such a community will individual rights be re-spected and the weak and helpless be protected. When the responsibilities of community membership are neglected, the rights of individuals, even if buttressed by ever more laws, become not only less secure but less satis-fying.

With its concern for individual rights and its suspicion of community morality, the liberal tradition has vested its confidence in procedural rules rather than ethical principles. The adversary process presupposes that the truth is most likely to emerge when opposing parties are represented by lawyers whose one goal is the vindication of their clients. The truth is pre-sumed to result from competition in the marketplace of ideas. If the truth is not sought by those committed to it, however, competing interests are not likely to disclose it. Lacking a supportive communal morality and as-sent to the spirit of the law, the legal system becomes coercive and bur-densome. Truth and justice are likely to be empty ideals—and finally to fade even as ideals—unless they are the acknowledged aim and purpose of the judicial process.[33] In order to justify the judicial and political system, they require commitment on the part of those involved; they presuppose a moral order affirmed by the society. Without it, justice is equated with le-gality, and society becomes more and more legalistic and litigious.

Moral Community and Pluralistic Society

The idea of American democracy as moral community would seem to fly in the face of the pluralistic character of the society. It seems to accord neither with the fact nor the ideal of democratic society. Some consider-ation needs to be given to the relation of pluralism and community.

Pluralism, and more particularly interest-group pluralism, is a promi-nent strand in current American ideology.[34] The theory of democratic plu-ralism developed as a response to the rise of industrial society and the problems it caused for classical democratic theory. In classical liberalism the citizen was related directly and immediately to the state. The emer-gence of mass politics and the displacement of family firms by large indus-trial corporations rendered that view obsolete. The citizen's relation to the state was now mediated through institutional associations. In addition to state and local governments and traditional voluntary associations, there are bureaucracies of government, business, and labor. Through the competition, bargaining, and accommodation of these interest groups, society is self-regulating, in this view.

The pluralistic theory of American democracy is reinforced by the heterogeneity of ethnic, religious, racial, and other groups. This diversity is protected by the legal separation of church and state and by the high value accorded to tolerance in the society. Robert Paul Wolff sums up the pluralistic view of America as "a complex interlocking of ethnic, religious, racial, regional, and economic groups, whose members pursue their diverse interests through the medium of private associations, which in turn are coordinated, regulated, contained, encouraged, and guided by a federal system of representative democracy."[35] How, then, can American democracy be understood as "moral community"?

That American society is pluralistic does not mean that it is therefore only a collectivity of atomistic individuals and interest groups. One of the early proponents of pluralist political science, E. Pendleton Herring, observed that while the "government of the democratic state reflects inescapably the underlying interest groups of society ... the very fact that the state exists evinces a basic community of purpose."[36] American democratic society is a pluralistic community.

Politics is not simply, and certainly not finally, a "play of power." It is also the pursuit of goods that citizens value as citizens and not merely as consumers. The good of the whole community includes the good of the whole self. In this view, "special interests" may be quite legitimate and at the same time limited and partial interests of the citizen. There are overriding interests that can be realized only by cooperation. The citizen will prize both the common interests of the community and the activity by which they are achieved.

It is easier to see how moral community accords with pluralistic society when we recognize that community entails both primary and inclusive relations. The notion of moral community extends the idea of community from that of the primary community of face-to-face relations to one of inclusive value meanings. For some, such as Albert Schweitzer, the most meaningful community has been that which embraces all of life, the very planet itself.

Only in this light can a community be kept open to that which transcends it. Otherwise, community will be an in-group, shut up to itself, closed to the possibility of change and growth, and hostile to all other groups, which will be seen as threats to its security. The two dimensions of community, primary and inclusive, are essentially, if dialectically, related. Each is nourished by the other, and each is checked and corrected by the other. Only if I am at home in my native community will I have the inner strength and transcending vision to seek the vague and intangible goods of the comprehensive community. And only if I have some vision of the inclusive community will I be sensitive to the provincialism and selfishness of the primary community and have the openness, the patience, and the courage to work for constructive change. Primary communities thus contribute to, constitute, and require the inclusive community of the pluralistic society.

Knowledge and Responsibility

Until the rise of modern technocracy, the individual was responsible to the community. But with technology, a structure was created with a life of its own—a legal-bureaucratic collectivity with the guiding ideals of objectivity, efficiency, and impersonality. The German industrialist Krupp, munitions manufacturer for Hitler during World War II, stated succinctly the goals of bureaucratization: "What I shall attempt to bring about is that nothing shall be dependent upon the life or existence of any particular person; that nothing of any importance shall happen or be caused to happen without the foreknowledge and approval of the management; that the past and the determinate future of the establishment can be learned in the files of the management without asking a question of any mortal."[37] Ethical responsibility becomes irrelevant.

When society is viewed objectively and theoretically, the individual seems to be lost from view. As mass society has encroached more and more on the individual, the notion of individuality has become increasingly privatized. The individual as the final court of moral authority, "subjective individualism," is a peculiarly modern notion, which has been intensified in direct proportion to the expansion of the powers of the political state and the technological society. Whether in the models of social systems or in analyses of social problems, the individual as an atom of the whole is insignificant. The scientific knowledge of societal forces, institutions, and trends appears to be remote from the lifeworld of the individual. Society and knowledge seem equally impersonal and alien to the self and its most immediate and pressing concerns.

In scientific theory or ethical analysis, one cannot think about society (the social system, the process of policy making) and the individual (personal responsibility) simultaneously. To attempt both is to become immobilized in thought. But to think one to the exclusion of the other is to falsify the reality. If knowledge of social issues and problems is the focus, the result is bound to be a personal sense of insignificance, impotence, and, finally, despair at the inability to affect or change "the System." If the values of the individual are the focus, a sense of unreality and irrelevance is likely to be the consequence because of the tenuous relation of values and ideals to the "real world," which has receded into the background.

Individual and society may be conceptually related by means of the "principle of complementarity." As both wave and particle theory are employed by the physicist to model atomic phenomena, so objective and subjective modes of analysis are required to understand the relation of ethics and policy making.[38] Not unlike the modern physicist, Kierkegaard developed his existential dialectic as a way of relating objectivity and subjectivity, abstract thought to concrete existence. Ethical inquiry traces moral responsibility to the individual. The normative question of what values should be decisive in the formation of public policy can only be answered by a person taking responsibility for the decision. When values are traced to the individual's lifeworld, they must be apprehended within that context through an act of sympathetic imagination or "indwelling."[39] And when such values are critically assessed and chosen as standards for decision making, the ethical principles by which they are justified must be affirmed by persons who take responsibility for them.

Subjectivity and objectivity appear to be diametrically opposed. Is not subjectivity arbitrary, relative, and idiosyncratic? Truth, in contrast, is generally viewed as objective, public, demonstrable. To ground ethics in subjectivity would seem to be to confine it to the private realm. But does this not create an unbridgeable chasm between the subjectivity of the private self and the objectivity of public policy?

The nature of subjectivity was illuminated by Kierkegaard in a way that secures his lasting significance as an ethical thinker. The Socratic-Kierkegaardian mode of thought is succinctly stated in Kierkegaard's formula "Subjectivity is truth." It is an insight quite at odds with the common notion of subjectivity. For him, as for Socrates, the most important truths were those that had to do with the *subject as a whole self,* the thinking, feeling, willing self in its historical existence.

To pose the ethical question *What is my personal relation to what I know?* is not to give warrant to "individualism" but to locate moral responsibility in the self. A public ethic represents in the first instance the creative and critical product of the reflection of an individual. It is social in context and meaning, but personal in judgment, decision, and responsibility. One begins with what is *given,* the presuppositions of the polity, the commonsense world and the commonsense notions and assumptions shared by citizens. The knower participates in the reality about which he or she inquires.

Democracy does not exist in a vacuum but in a particular history. To understand American democracy we have to locate it in our story, as shaped by our struggles to survive, to be free, and to attain a better life. We have to see it as the way this moral community seeks to govern itself. Democracy must be more than majority rule and minority rights, more than constitutional checks and balances and representative government, more than merely rules of the game. Democracy must presuppose a commitment to justice and the common good, values, and ideals rooted in our shared history. Events in that history continue to resonate with moral meaning for our lives. Earth Day is one.

Earth Day

During the 1960s, trying simultaneously to build the Great Society and to wage war in Vietnam, the United States was engaged in an extraordinary effort to land a man on the moon by the end of the decade. The eyes of Americans were focused abroad and above. But something happened to our perception of ourselves with the actual landing on the moon in July 1969. For the first time, we were able to look at ourselves from another planet. The picture of planet earth, fragile and ethereal, wreathed in clouds and floating in space, had a poignant beauty that made it at once a symbol of our global interdependence, with each other and with the earth. The contrast of the sterile moon, devoid of air, water, and life, with an earth rich in resources but vulnerable to despoliation and without external resources other than solar radiation, made people aware of the need for conservation of the world.

Perils to the environment were becoming evident on a wide scale. The world's oceans were dumping grounds for noxious wastes; air over the cities was being polluted with carbon dioxide; the land was becoming contaminated with toxic chemicals and radioactive wastes. Conservation forces mobilized, and on 22 April 1970, with the support of President Richard Nixon and with congressional leadership, the United States celebrated Earth Day. Organizers of Earth Day enlisted the efforts of thousands of colleges, grammar and high schools, and over 2000 citizen groups in communities across the nation. Young volunteers of the Environmental Action Coalition organized and planned the events of Earth Day in a four-month interval between January and April, 1970, on a budget of only $125,000.[40]

The nation responded in demonstrations against the threats to the environment in an unprecedented way. In New York City, for one full day five midtown city blocks were closed to vehicular traffic so that over 100 educational exhibits on the problems of pollution could be held in the streets.[41] New York City Mayor John Lindsay showed symbolic support for the day, as did many other public officials throughout the nation, by riding only on mass transit or in electric cars.[42] Governor Nelson Rockefeller of New York signed a bill to help control pollution and encourage conservation. The citizens of New York City gathered for at least three separate rallies at Union Square, and a quarter of a million strong assembled on Manhattan's Fourteenth Street. There were massive assemblies elsewhere in the country; Congress found it necessary to recess because so many of its members were participating in Earth Day programs outside of the capital. Earth Day prompted other important measures, such as New Jersey Governor William T. Cahill's decision to create a state department of environmental protection. The National Education Association estimated that 10 million public school children were involved in Earth Day "teach-ins." [43]

Earth Day was a dramatic and effective exercise in a collective, national process of ethical reflection. In the words of Earth Day planners, it was "a day to re-examine the ethic of individual progress at mankind's expense—a day to challenge the corporate and governmental leaders who promise change, but who shortchange the necessary programs ... April 22 [sought and continues to seek] a future worth living." [44] What difference, then, has it made in our national life?

Since 1970, Earth Day has been observed on 21 March in the United States and abroad by those wishing to call attention to the problems of the world's deteriorating natural environment. [45]

The magnitude and spirit of Earth Day 1970 were not matched until Earth Day 1990. In retrospect, however, it seems clear that the trend of increasing environmental awareness and of symbolic events such as Earth Day in the late 1960s and early 1970s had a very real impact on the formulation of governmental policy. Indeed, after just two short years of ironing out the details, Congress passed the Clean Water Act of 1972, which brought stiff new regulations to control pollution of streams and help fund their cleanup. Other governmental policy reactions followed. [46]

Projected benefits of the 1972 wave of environmental legislation in the wake of Earth Day have fallen short of some hoped-for results. While the Clean Water Act, for example, did improve the quality of some 36,000 stream miles across the United States, it let a 1985 deadline for the "stoppage" of point-source pollution come and go unheeded. With the move into the 1980s, the new national policy trend was to transfer federally enacted environmental policy from federal to state and private levels. Indicative of the trend of federal disengagement was the 1986 Reagan-sponsored program "Take Pride in America," set up to reward states, private corporations, and other groups symbolically for their attempts at addressing environmental concerns. [47]

Aside from these amorphous and largely impotent federal measures, state and local governments are still making keen efforts to improve the environment. Some states, such as Massachusetts and Iowa, have passed rigorous antipollution laws, though most states, for example Florida and

New Jersey, do not address environmental problems until they pose a serious and immediate threat.[48]

Symbol and Reality

By the 1990s, it was clear that Earth Day was not a transitory phenomenon. Scientists were beginning to warn that the buildup of gases emitted from fossil fuels, if unaltered, would heat up the earth, creating a greenhouse effect that would make the planet unlivable within seventy-five years. Climate shifts would occur over decades, not over millions of years, as has been the case until now. Although scientists still do not agree as to how the greenhouse effect will affect us, they are more and more certain that changes will be portentous. One of the most disturbing facts is that the changes now showing up are the result of what happened thirty years ago. The crisis is still largely invisible.

In addition to the rise in global temperatures caused by the dumping of massive quantities of gases into the atmosphere, there is conclusive evidence of a huge hole in the earth's ozone layer, on which life depends for protection from deadly ultraviolet radiation. There were new fears of environmental degradation with the Alaskan oil spill in March 1989. The *Exxon Valdez* went aground, pouring 10 million gallons into Prince William Sound, with the prospect of catastrophic damage to the coastline and to sea life. The contamination caused untold deaths of sea otters, salmon and herring, tufted puffins and eagles, deer, bears, wolves, bighorn sheep, and caribou, with critical effects on Alaska's fishing, tourism, oil drilling, and logging industries. Destruction of the world's forests is taking place at the rate of an area the size of Tennessee every year. More than half of all living species may be wiped out within our lifetimes. Every day, crop failures and political fiascos are responsible for 37,000 deaths by starvation or preventable diseases of children under the age of five.

Earth Day is a potent symbol for the dawning realization that people now living hold in their hands the fate of our imperiled planet. In order to meet the challenge of the environmental crisis, profound changes will have to take place. Actions will have to be taken at the global level, but they cannot begin there. They can only originate from a widespread consciousness of global interdependence and shared responsibility for the earth. Americans may begin to discover the wisdom of the Indian Chief Seattle, who said in a speech in 1854, "The earth does not belong to man; man belongs to the earth." Translated into action, that awareness can change our lives. Without it, environmental ethics remains an abstraction.

Events and movements such as the student vigil and Earth Day, one at the local level and the other embracing the globe, represent a new political vision. No longer can citizens wait for government to act, or for political leaders to lead. Effective and lasting results will come from citizens who start where they are, engage in grass-roots political activity, and in so doing find common cause with multitudes of others. The enterprise of ethics should be oriented to this end.

To undertake ethical analysis is to engage in a critique of culture. Our aim in this inquiry is to understand.[49] But to understand the situation is to transform it, for self-understanding leads to action. In seeking to ask the right questions, we may find some clues in posing the ethical question as *What is my personal relation to what I know?* We are trying to deepen our understanding, as a means to intelligent action. We seek to discover and recover what we know at the deepest levels of our personal being and social existence: that we are persons in community and that the meaning and quality of our lives require a moral context. But can we assume that society as we know it today has a communal dimension? We must consider the relation of community to society, historically and in the present.

2

COMMUNITY, SOCIETY, AND ETHICS

HE PRESUMPTION that fact and value can be cleanly separated and the attempt to develop a value-free social theory are rooted in the intellectual history of modernity. Only an observer from another time and place could fully appreciate the irony of a value-free description of society professed by social theorists who are themselves driven by the values of that society. As long as the regnant values of industrial American society were taken for granted, social ethics was assumed to be unnecessary (because of continuing technological and social advance), impossible (because of the loss of a common religious and moral worldview) and undesirable (because of the danger of imposing a particular morality on a pluralistic society). But there are public policy issues that as value choices cannot possibly be solved through scientific or technological rationality alone. Problems such as the bankruptcies of small and middle-size farms, the need for job training for the unemployed, help for poor single-parent families, a long-range energy policy, and other public policy issues require the exercise of social ethics.

The questions of ethics arise within a particular ethos, or way of life, that distinguishes one group from others. The possibility and character of a social ethic depend on its communal and societal ethos. Its meaning must be understood within a form of life, its own ethos, before its claim to validity can be rightly assessed. The ethos of modern industrial society differs from that of earlier societies, and of medieval community in particular, in the quality of communal life experienced by its members.

Medieval Community and the Rise of Modernity

The ethos of the medieval world was community. The "great chain of being" stretched from peasantry to papacy to the throne of God. Obligations and privileges, duties and rights, were defined in a social hierarchy infused with religious meaning. Thomas Aquinas had written that everyone included in a community stood in relation to that community "as parts to the whole." Man was distinguished from other creatures by his capacity "to know the truth about God and to live in communities." That view of the nature of man was characteristic of medieval society. Persons were highly valued in the eyes of the church and found meaning in the communal life of village, guild, and feudal class. Though diversified and decentralized, it was a generally stable society.

Historians agree on two social characteristics of the Middle Ages: the preeminence of the small social group and the importance of status in society. Just as the ancient Hebrew had known himself to be the son of Abraham, Isaac, and Jacob (as Yahweh was "the God of Abraham, Isaac, and Jacob"), so the identity of medieval man was defined by his membership and role as an intrinsic part of the whole religious order of things. Within that order, varieties of Christian virtues and human vices were exhibited, along with technology and economic activity.[1] Canon law endorsed serfdom, and the church was part of the whole system of feudal exploitation. The economic thought inherited by the sixteenth century was conservative. Medieval writers were much taken up with discussions of money, prices, and interest, in particular of the just price and the prohibition of usury.[2] Practice belied Christian ideals—the church exemplified the worst as well as the best in the period—but ultimately all human activity, individual and social, was subject to ethical standards. The ethical norms of the church were acknowledged by the society, however often or grievously those norms might be violated.

During the Middle Ages, forces were at work that would later transform communal society. Capital cities were growing and trade was expanding, raising the horizons of men and leveling barriers between people and classes. Interest in scientific knowledge was awakening, and the state was assuming more importance in the spheres of commerce, science, the military, and the law. Along with changing social and economic conditions came new ways of thinking that would constitute a radically different worldview.

Individualism made a dramatic debut on the stage of modern history with the secular Renaissance and the beginning of the Protestant Reformation. The Reformation retained a link with the medieval church through the internalization of religious life and at the same time marked a rupture with the medieval world. The dynamic impulse of a personal faith fostered by a new understanding of the biblical message led Martin Luther to challenge the sale of indulgences. In pressing the logic of salvation by grace through faith, Luther rejected the entire sacramental system of the Roman Catholic church and finally the authority of the pope himself. It was one man's faith pitted against the dogma of the church. Religious individualism thus made its appearance, though its audacious challenge to the church succeeded only through the protection of secular rulers. Individualism and nationalism were together a new and portentous combination.

The emergence of the individual, distinct within community and self-contained, marks the beginnings of modern society. The individual was preeminently represented in the trader and the scientific thinker. Trade was the incentive and example for all forms of social life[3] (a fact of the greatest importance for modern self-understanding, as we later see). Just as the trader moved outward toward new horizons, so the powers of the individual mind extended the boundaries of the natural world. The thinker turned from the contemplation of the spiritual world to the solid reality of the external world, whose physical appearance was now the object of intense interest. An earth-centered universe gave way to the sun-centered universe of Copernicus and Galileo. Nominalism eclipsed the philosophy of Platonic realism: reality consisted in things themselves, not in some ideal form or heavenly pattern. The method of scientific induction supplanted the authority of tradition. The first step in Francis Bacon's scientific program was to be an "expurgation of the intellect"; in like fashion, Descartes was shortly to base philosophy on radical doubt; John Locke would describe the mind as a blank tablet to be inscribed with the perceptions of the external world. The individual scientist was charting the path of the future.

The Science to Come

Bacon expressed in himself and in his work the aims of the science to come: the unity of knowledge, the empirical method, value-free objectivity, the use of scientific technique for the control and exploitation of nature, the utilitarian meaning of truth. Bacon was the prototype of the modern thinker in the way in which he linked knowledge and power throughout his writings. Early in the seventeenth century, Bacon announced the intent of his work, *Instauratio Magna* (The Great Renewal), with themes that were to be dominant motifs in the social theory of the next three centuries: "I am laboring to lay the foundation not of any sect or doctrine, but of human utility and power."[4]

The paradigm of the new scientific method was mathematics. Kepler, claiming the authority of Aristotle, asserted that the mind could know nothing but quantities. Galileo declared that philosophy (i.e., "natural philosophy," or science) was written in "the grand book of the universe . . . in the language of mathematics." Nature was a Great Machine in the view of Descartes: "Give me extension and motion, and I will construct the universe," he boasted. The beauty of the world now lay in its elegant symmetry, its regularity and precision, its clocklike workings. Gone were purpose, the qualities of taste, smell, color (the "secondary" qualities of Galileo), and all that gave human meaning to the universe. The knowledge of the new science of Descartes and Newton was purged of its personal characteristics.

The origins of social science, and of its utilitarian character, lie in seventeenth- and eighteenth-century natural science. Natural science was the model for philosophy and the new science of politics, to which Hobbes applied the assumptions of Galileo and Descartes about extension and motion and the distinction between primary and secondary qualities. Thomas Hobbes and John Locke brought to their respective political works, *Leviathan* and *Two Treatises of Government,* a resolutely empirical approach that rejected all appeals to history and tradition. Both Hobbes and Locke began in their political theorizing with the atomistic unit of the self-interested individual; the problem was how essentially separate individuals, with private and conflicting interests, could coexist in tolerable harmony.

The most fundamental feature of Hobbes and Locke, certainly the most significant for subsequent social theory, was their atomistic individ-

ualism. Instead of taking a historical view of man and society, they began
with an original state of nature and with society as a mass of atoms. In this
they reflected the ethos of their time. In the period of Renaissance, Reformation, and the beginnings of capitalist economy, there began to emerge
the concept of "the individual" abstracted from the complex of relationships by which he had been defined in the medieval community. "The
counterpart of this process," says Raymond Williams, "was a similar abstraction of 'society.' "[5] Whereas society had earlier signified actual personal relationships, in the late sixteenth century it began to assume the
more general and modern meaning of "the system of common life."

The framework and central themes of the liberal tradition were established in terms of the model of society as a collection of atomistic individuals, in contrast to the community of persons that had earlier been the regnant image. The revolutions of the eighteenth and nineteenth centuries all
contributed in fact and theory to the eclipse of person-in-community by
individual-in-society.

The Economic Revolution

The drama of the American and French revolutions has tended to eclipse a
less obvious but equally fundamental change that was taking place—the
economic revolution. Political and economic revolutions proceeded apace:
In the same year, 1776, the Declaration of Independence was proclaimed
in the colonies and Adam Smith's *Wealth of Nations* was published in Britain. Both the word *industry,* indicating an economic institution, and *democracy,* as a political institution, can be dated from this time.[6] Capitalism had
been growing in Europe, but it lacked a philosophy. Certainly the idea of
personal gain was not new, but now the theory of a system organized on
the basis of the free action of profit-seeking men in a market took root,
and an economic world began to be distinguished from the social world as
a separate and self-contained realm.[7]

Liberty and property were two sides of the same coin in the thought
of John Locke. "The great and chief end of men uniting into common-
wealths and putting themselves under government," declared Locke, "is
the preservation of their property." The Founding Fathers were landed

gentlemen; the American Revolution was begun and controlled by the up-
per class. Adam Smith himself had observed that behind legal and constitutional arguments was the real fight for position and power. "The leading
men of America, like those of all countries," he said in *Wealth of Nations,*
"desire to preserve their own importance."[8]

Increasingly, political freedom was conceived predominantly in terms
of economic individualism. Hobbes had stripped away the intermediate associations between individual and state, family, guild, church—the whole
complex of customs, traditions, and moralities that infused life with meaning, purpose, and security—in order to protect and foster the individual's
freedom to pursue his own ends. With the rise of the Industrial Revolution in England, Hobbes's theory became a grim and brutal reality. Com-
mons land was expropriated and enclosed by lords of the manor. Communal property became private property, and the yeoman, driven off his land,
became a poor laborer or tenant, a beggar or a robber. Men were forced
from the village into the industrial town, where they became a source of
cheap labor. Now the market economy became both the sphere and the
guarantor of individual freedom for the middle class, though, as Karl
Polanyi has pointed out, laissez-faire economy was not "natural"; it was
the product of deliberate state intervention.[9]

By the mid-nineteenth century, economics had come to be seen as an
autonomous world, distinct from the social and political, governed by the
inexorable laws of nature. For Adam Smith, economics had been a human
science; moral community and national life still provided the standards of
good and evil. Whereas for Smith the self-interest of individuals was
guided by the providential hand for the good of the society as a whole and
economic activity was only a part of the society and subject to its moral restraints and standards, for Jeremy Bentham laissez-faire economics was
justified by utility alone.

During the 1830s when economic liberalism became a militant cru-
sade, utilitarians saw it as a program that would produce the greatest happiness for the greatest number. In spite of the misery it brought to millions
of the British lower class, the Industrial Revolution inspired utopian visions of affluence, which held the promise of gratifying man's wants. Jeremy Bentham was indefatigable in his efforts for social reform, no matter if
some of his schemes were far-fetched (such as his desires to legislate for

India and to rule Mexico) or morally dubious (such as Panopticon, a prison to be run for profit, which he defined as a "mill for grinding rogues honest, and idle men industrious").[10] He applied the standard of utility in drawing up comprehensive codes of penal and constitutional law and in his efforts to rationalize and strengthen the administrative agency of government. Economic success required inclination, knowledge, and power; only the state could supply the necessary knowledge and power. A strong centralized state was not the antithesis but the corollary of individualism for Bentham; the state represented the will of the whole people. Even though Bentham's crude pleasure-pain psychology was refined by John Stuart Mill and the Idealist Utilitarians, his program for the application of social science to the field of public policy proved him to be a man of the future, for better or worse.

Morality and the Marketplace

In precapitalist society, religion provided the social cohesion and transcendent moral standards for the social, political, and economic life of the community. In the capitalist era, the internalization of the Protestant ethic not only gave moral sanction to the marketplace, it provided the indirect social controls that restrained immoral behavior. At the least, it consecrated wealth to social use when it had accumulated beyond the capacity of its maker to use or to take with him beyond the grave. As Protestant man was replaced by profit-maximizing man, the sanctions and restraints of social morality diminished.

The internalization of the moral standards of the Protestant ethic acted as an indirect control of capitalism in its early stage. Within the ethos of the Protestant ethic, "enterprise" had moral significance: hard work, rational planning, and prudence characterized the man who devoted himself to the worldly "calling" of business. The work ethic was complemented with the ruling class's paternalism, a sense of obligation to the needy and a regard for the code of honor and service. But the rise of utilitarianism brought about a change in the thought world of capitalism. It reflected the Enlightenment view of man as a rational being. Since self-interest was rational, in a harmonious world ruled by reason, self-interest and altruism would arrive at the same end. The utilitarian-consumerist notion of the individual eliminated moral philosophy from the social plane. The market was neutral and amoral. Collective goods were equated with individual goods. Morality was now confined to the private sphere.

The pursuit of individual interests in the marketplace operated to effect the general interest "as by an invisible hand," in Adam Smith's world of free enterprise. But Smith was realistic about the motives and behavior of merchants and recognized the need for restraint of monopoly and other forms of activity that impaired the self-regulating mechanism of the market. The growth of capitalism brought problems necessitating governmental intervention in the marketplace. The increase in the number and size of monopolies, the abuse of the consumer, and the degradation of the environment made governmental controls imperative. Collective bargaining power and greater activity by organized groups disturbed the traditional operation of the market in distributing rewards according to effort.

Such contradictions within its own theory and historical development led to a crisis in modern capitalism. Its justification in theory had rested on the economic ground of efficiency of production and, in the early stages, of the bourgeois morality that connected economic reward with moral virtue. But with the loss of that morality, what incentives were there for the individual to restrain self-interest in the interests of the society as a whole? Why should individuals adopt moral standards by which to judge and restrain their behavior if the system as such could not be validated by moral criteria? With the transition to a managed economy, there was greater need of a supporting moral ethos and ethical justification of the economic system, but as economic individualism was growing as an ideology, social morality was eroding.

Modern Society and Social Theory

With the dissolution of traditional ties of medieval community, the individual was liberated to stand alone, with a sense both of new powers and of greater vulnerability to forces of the marketplace. The common social world was divided into autonomous realms of science, religion, economics, and politics, each seen as self-regulating. The rise of the scientific outlook brought a new way of looking at the world, as an alien reality bereft of human meaning but subject to human control. Human reason was conceived more and more as technical rationality, limited to calculation of the most efficient means, leaving ends or purposes to individual preference. The common standard of value became utility, seen successively as happiness, pleasure, individual interest, and money. Value was sundered from fact, eliminated from the realms of science and economics and, in the political realm, equated with individual interest. It is against the background of these developments that modern social theory is to be understood. We may then see why it is is difficult to raise the ethical question in the public realm.

The pathfinding thinkers of the Enlightenment could take for granted the moral-communal background of social life, no matter how critical their theories might be of the social bonds of community, authority, and religion. Adam Smith is a notable example. The moral assumptions that underlay his *Wealth of Nations* had been made quite explicit in Smith's earlier treatise, *The Theory of Moral Sentiments*. Man was a social creature, moved by his egoism but also by altruism. Utility was only one of the four sources of moral approval, the last and least. Sympathy was the basis of morality. The capacity for fellow feeling, mutuality, and the desire for social approval enabled the individual to assume the point of view of the "Impartial Spectator," which represented both the general moral standards of society and individual conscience. Smith believed the moral nature of man to be grounded in nature itself (he sought to apply the methods of Newtonian science to morality), but his moral man was the British middle-class image of the perfect gentleman. Social convention, propriety, and respect for the moral rules of the game restrained the individual in his pursuit of self-interest.[11]

The Loss of Community in Utilitarianism

The moral community presupposed by Adam Smith disappeared in later utilitarianism. In economics and in liberal political theory, the individual was treated as an autonomous unity, interchangeable with other discrete entities, without essential connection with others. The community, declared Jeremy Bentham, "is a fictitious body, composed of the individual persons who are considered as constituting as it were its members."[12]

Utilitarianism expressly combined science and morality, the science based on the purported laws of individual self-interest, the morality based on a method of satisfying individual interests. The idea of moral good that is essentially communal, a concern for the good of the neighbor, is transposed into a nonmoral good, pleasure, or happiness. Morality is reduced to individual desires, preferences, which are enshrined as "utilities" in the science of economics.

The notion of *utility,* central to the rise of modern science from the time of Francis Bacon, provided a way of fusing morality, social science, and public policy, for "utility" seemed to be both a scientific concept and a self-evident good. Hobbes's social theory, Talcott Parsons has said, "is almost a pure case of utilitarianism."[13] It displays what Parsons notes as the four major characteristics of utilitarianism: atomism, rationality, empiricism, and the randomness of ends, all connected with the economic doctrine of utility.[14]

Bentham acknowledged that it was David Hume who had taught him "that *utility* was the test and measure of all virtue." "Utility," said Hume, was "the *sole* source of that high regard paid to justice, fidelity, honour, allegiance and chastity ... it is a foundation of the chief part of morals, which has a reference to mankind and to our fellow-creatures."[15] Bentham, like Hobbes and Hume, saw reason as essentially "reckoning" or calculating. Knowledge was a utility, a means to power. Later in his life, Bentham began to use the term "happiness" for utility and pronounced the "sacred truth" that "the greatest happiness of the greatest number is the foundation of morals and legislation."[16] By adopting the principle of the greatest happiness of the greatest number, the utilitarians were able to create a political philosophy based on utility as the measure of social morality.

Utilitarian theory confines rationality to the means-end relationship and leaves the question and character of ends to the individual. Ends are subjective, random choices of the individual. Rationality devises the most appropriate and effective means of achieving the desired end. Rationality is instrumental, not substantive; morality is individual and subjective. The "greatest happiness of the greatest number" is simply the sum of individual preferences. In the substitution of "happiness" for "utility," there is a subtle but important shift from the idea of utility as a *means* (use) to that of an *end* (happiness). If utility (means) is replaced by "happiness of the greatest number" (end), how is that end to be rationally determined, and why should the self-interested individual seek it?

The Problem of Order in Utilitarianism

The question of how atomistic individuals governed by their competitive self-interest can live together in a state of peace, the "Hobbesian problem of order," has continued to plague utilitarian thought for 200 years.[17] Given the scarcity of goods, an unlimited struggle for power, the restriction of rationality to the means necessary to achieve what one desires, and the impossibility of reaching reasoned agreement about the ends of life, utilitarianism has had difficulty in finding a satisfactory alternative to the authoritarian state. The centralization of state power was necessary, in Bentham's view, in order to effect social reform rationally and efficiently. Given the utilitarian assumptions of atomistic individualism, egoism, and instrumental rationality, freedom was seen as liberation from custom, tradition, indeed, the whole network of social relationships. Only a powerful rational state could guarantee that kind of individual freedom.

Whereas Hobbes thought that the anarchic impulses of hedonistic individuals could be restrained only by a powerful state (with the ruler limited by his prudent recognition of the limitations of his power and the need to rule in the best interests of his subjects), most utilitarians since have adopted some form of Locke's postulate of the rational recognition of the "natural identity of interests."[18] Enlightened self-interest would coincide with the interests of the society as a whole. The normative order consisted of a social contract entailing only minimal governmental powers. There was no need to seek rational agreement on the ends of society, for in classical economic theory individuals could use one another as means to their own ends, to mutual advantage, in exchange of services and possessions. Private vice would be transposed into public virtue, as Adam Smith believed, through the operation of the "invisible hand" in the marketplace.

In Britain the utilitarian society and its philosophers, Hume, Bentham, James Mill, and John Stuart Mill, evoked substantial critical response from the moral philosophers T.H. Green, F.H. Bradley, and others,[19] who criticized the atomistic individualism of utilitarianism and the naturalistic substitution of pleasure and utility for morality and obligation. They affirmed the social nature of man and sought to reestablish his place in the universe. Though they stressed man's social relations, their idealist ethical theory was abstract; they failed to relate man's moral life to the kind of social existence peculiar to modern industrial society. Karl Marx was in agreement with Hegel and the British idealists on the communal basis of life, but because the communal society had given way to the market society, he believed that morality should be recognized as a bourgeois ideology that cloaked class interests. Radical criticism was to be directed to the economic institutions that alienated man from others and from himself.

The Pioneers of Sociology

Modern sociology traces its origins to nineteenth-century thinkers who combined in varying degrees a preoccupation with the methods of the new science and a reaction to the loss of community in the new industrial society. The themes of community, authority and the sacred were prominent in the thought of Auguste Comte, Alexis de Tocqueville, Ferdinand Toennies, Max Weber, Emile Durkheim, and Georg Simmel, who saw in modern industrial society forces at work dissolving communal ties, resulting in anonymity, impersonality, competition and conflict, and alienation. In tracing the development of modern society from community, Toennies stressed two interrelated trends: the increasing importance of reason, law, and large-scale organization and the accompanying deterioration of the personal and moral quality of life. Max Weber, the most influential of the social theorists after Toennies, followed much the same line of thought in his penetrating analysis of developing industrial society. In his view, the Protestant Reformation and the French Revolution marked the pivotal points in the historic shift in Western society from medieval communalism to centralized government organized on the basis of "rational-legal" authority. The community as the locus of life dissolved in the corrosive acids of economic individualism and the rationalization of all spheres of life, represented most significantly (and ominously) in the ever-expanding bureaucratization of life.

By the close of the nineteenth century, the results of unbridled economic individualism and the growth of big business in America evoked protests of various kinds. American sociology in its beginnings combined a moral concern with a sense of nostalgia for the rapidly disappearing communal life found in the village and on the frontier. The pioneers of American sociology were for the most part rural born and raised, as were some of the leading social philosophers, such as Josiah Royce.[20]

Progressive thinkers opposed the liberal, utilitarian society of the Gilded Age with communitarian ideals and programs ranging from the metaphysical communal philosophy of Royce to plans for restructuring society along communitarian lines. Men as different as Charles Horton Cooley, Herbert Croly, W. E. B. Du Bois, and John Dewey all wrestled with the problem of how people could regain a sense of common purpose and of political control over their own lives.[21] The solution remained elusive, however; the tenacious liberal commitment to economic self-interest, the self-regulating market and the "natural identity of interests" overcame the quest for communal purposes, loyalties, and institutions. Charles Peirce might argue that truth, and James Mark Baldwin that morality, depended on community; Henry Adams might look back to the ideal existence of community in medieval France and Edward Bellamy look forward to its utopian form in A.D. 2000; the fact was that the growth of the organizational state with its complex economic and political forces seemed to be rendering the individual insignificant and community chimerical. Jackson Wilson concludes his study of social philosophy spanning the turn of the century with the words: "There probably *was* no form of community which could be efficient and powerful enough to cope with modern America and still be spiritually bound together by what Peirce called love and Royce loyalty."[22]

Social thinkers have viewed this development of Western history variously. Some have focused on the alienation resulting from the loss of community, while others have celebrated liberation from the suffocating bonds of traditional community. Weber's pessimism about the process of rationalization has not been shared by such sociologists as Talcott Parsons, who take an optimistic view of the process as one that is widening rather than restricting social and political freedom.[23]

There is a pervasive ambivalence in the reflections of social critics on the achievements of modern society. At the very moment when those in the Western world seemed about to attain the fullest realization of the great liberal ideals of freedom and reason, some historical ironies manifested themselves. It is not simply, as Erich Fromm said some forty years ago, that the freedom of modern man "has brought him independence and rationality," it has also "made him isolated and, thereby, anxious and powerless."[24] How did it transpire that freedom and reason could come not simply to function as supreme moral ideals but finally to take the place of morality itself and to issue not in a fully human society but in a world that appears to defy human control? Max Weber's prophecy[25] seems to many contemporary social critics to be borne out by the unfolding logic of the technological society: The inexorable process of rationalization has undermined the nonrational basis of morality, which is rooted in community and personal relations.

Community as a Form of Social Thought

The quest for community in simple, preindustrial terms is doomed to frustration. But the persistence of the communal theme in the writings of social and political theorists testifies to its continuing significance. Community is one of the "fundamental forms of social thought."[26] Conservative social theorists employ *community* as a root metaphor; liberal and radical theorists, the metaphor of *society*.[27] The liberal paradigm assumes the society metaphor but differs from the radical stance in taking for granted the institutional structures of society; radical social theory subjects them to thoroughgoing criticism. One might say that the ethical imperative of conservatism is that things ought to be the way they were; for radicalism, things ought to be the way they will be; for liberalism, things ought to be the way they are.

Liberals who undertake to go beyond description to prescription are at a loss for conceptual categories adequate to the task, for their dependence on the unstable combination of the assumptions of economic individualism and welfare statism give them no grounds for critical transcendence of the society as it exists. Indeed, the problem is more fundamental: They have no grounds for value judgment at all. By assuming a separation between description ("fact") and prescription ("value"), they undercut any basis for anything they would say in prescription.

Conservatives can denounce society from the perspective of the ideal of moral community, but without breaking with classical economic liberalism (the core of modern conservatism), they are unable to offer much more than a utopian appeal to adopt a pure form of laissez-faire capitalism. Radicals attack capitalism with moral fervor; their critique of institutional structures and processes is often penetrating and difficult to refute. In "unmasking" morality, however, they cannot account for their own moral passion or give more than an ideological (class-interest bound) explanation of society, which must include the critics themselves. But the critiques of conservatism and radicalism are often more interesting, relevant, and important than those of liberalism because of the relative moral complacency of liberalism. This is in part because of the tendency in liberalism to shift the ground of public choice from morality to technical rationality through its use of the utilitarian calculus.

Utilitarianism does not figure prominently as a distinct movement in ethics today.[28] But incorporated in social science, it has achieved a kind of implicit moral autonomy, combining the value-free ideal of the pursuit of knowledge for its own sake with its value as an instrument of human betterment.[29] Utilitarianism, like Marxism and Freudianism, has aspired to rigorous objectivity while cloaking the moral passion that has energized it and that has constituted much of its appeal. Since the eighteenth century, observes Michael Polanyi, we have seen "many hardened utilitarians nobly upholding their logically unaccountable moral convictions—but only in the twentieth century has popular thought been permeated by this internal contradiction."[30] Utilitarianism has neglected the moral context within which respect for persons and for one's obligations and promises weighs more heavily than the notion of utility. "Utility does indeed have a place in our practical reasoning," argues the philosopher A.I. Melden, "but only against an existing moral background, which, being background, is all too easily lost to view."[31] Seemingly objective and value-free societal systems of thought grow out of communal life and sustain their appeal and legitimacy in part at least because of their tacit dependence upon their moral background. It is essential, however, to acknowledge the continuing communal dimension of society because it constitutes the irreducibly human, the moral, quality of life. It is the necessary foundation for an ethical determination of public policy. Only a social theory that recognizes the com-

mon roots of knowledge and value in community can admit the possibility
of social ethics.

Communal Society?

The sociologist Daniel Bell describes contemporary American society as a
"communal society" because of its functional interdependence. But since
it lacks a communal ethic, the society is unable to deal adequately with its
large-scale problems.[32] By pushing his analysis to an examination of the
"cultural contradictions of capitalism,"[33] Bell is led to conclude that only a
"public philosophy" can ensure political pursuit of the ideals of justice and
the common good. One wonders, however, how a public philosophy is
possible on the basis of a liberal view of society that leaves unchallenged
the objectivistic conception of knowledge and tends to equate value with
the subjective preferences of individuals.

The social theorist does not simply theorize about something "out
there" but brings a conception of society to the investigation of social facts.
That conception cannot be verified in any strictly empirical test, though it
can be validated in reference to a broad range of human experience. If a
social theory is to be adequate both as description of empirical reality and
as a context for moral judgment, it will have to give an account of the
communal dimension to society.

Industrial society is a "communal society" not only because of the
functional interdependence of its members but also because of the moral
quality of their mutual relations. These relations presuppose respect for
persons, honesty and truthfulness, a reasonable degree of trust in others,
compassion for those who hurt or are in need, a willingness to do one's
part in a common enterprise. In a communal society persons will, at least
on occasion, put family, work, aid to others, or service to the wider community above the immediate concerns of self-interest. These are not
saintly or heroic ideals; they are the qualities that give meaning and value
to ordinary life and that inform public policy intended to meet human
needs.

Social theory that treats the human being as an individual-in-society
to the neglect of person-in-community fails on two counts. First, it does

not do justice to the dialectic of community and society that can be traced through Western history. Second, it does not do justice to the dialectical character of human nature reflected in the historical dialectic of community and society.

Although the principles of community and society are embodied in sequential epochs, they are also ever-present in dialectical tension.[34] Community is primary, and society is itself the creature of community. However superordinate the impersonal relations in certain institutions, were there no modicum of community, there would be no society. We would all be "windowless monads" (Leibnitz). The dialectical relation of community (direct, intimate relations) and society (indirect, impersonal relations) that we can trace in the development of the modern West is present also in the self-reflective experience of the individual. The ethical dialectic is generated in the tension between one's experience as person-in-community and as individual-in-society.

The Ethical Dialectic of Community and Society

A reconsideration of the nature of social ethics as generated in the ethical dialectic of community and society will not lead to the reconstitution of society. It may, however, result in a clearer understanding of the contribution that ethical thought can make to public policy. It may disclose the desirability and the reality of a common morality; it may also indicate the possibility and limitations of ethical reasoning. Such reflection may encourage a greater confidence in our capacities to relate to others as fellow human beings. And it may disclose possibilities for the education of civic-minded citizens. All of this suggests the need to trace the dialectic of ethical reasoning to the nature of persons as both communal and self-interested.

The social dialectic of community and society seen in the dependence of capitalism and utilitarianism on the communal ground of modern society has its analogue in the ethical dialectic. Community and society as two conceptually distinct forms of life reflect the dialectic of ethical thought. One is a person-in-community, sharing values with others, related by kinship or fellowship or common loyalty; one is also an individual-in-society, with interests of one's own. No matter how rational, the person is bound by affectional ties to family, neighbors, and friends. But in normal moral development individuals reach a point at which they begin to subject the morality of their community to reasoned criticism. The development of individuality as well as of modern civilization itself requires the rational criticism of morality. That ethic nevertheless requires a moral and hence communal ground. The ethical question *What is my personal relation to what I know?* is a dialectic characterized by three polarities.

INDIVIDUAL AND GROUP

The first of these polarities is the relation between individual and group. A view of the individual as an isolated, independent entity in society limits ethics to a "morality of self-interest."[35] Hedonistic and utilitarian ethics fail to account for the moral obligation to seek the good of others. But when we recognize the fundamental fact of moral community, the co-presence of the self and the other, the problem of relating self-interest to the interests of others is transposed to a different level. It is then not so much a question of philosophical theory as of the capacity and intent of the imagination and will: What do I see? and What am I to do? Moral philosophy has here a different though important role to play in critical analysis and constructive guidance of moral reason.[36]

The philosophical debate over the question What is "moral"? is difficult if not impossible to resolve unless there is agreement on the principle of respect for persons. Moral obligation consists of the duty to respect and care for other persons with whom one's own existence is bound up. We share a common world and owe one another the recognition of "inalienable human rights" because we exist and fulfill our potential in response to one another. The presence of the other constitutes a claim on my life because that presence is a condition of my own existence. I actualize my own personhood as I enter into personal relations with others.[37] A proper understanding of justice and the common good must begin with a view of the person as a responsive and responsible self, in a community of other selves. The place to begin in understanding the way we think and value is not with Descartes's *Cogito ergo sum,* but with the more realistic *Respondeo, ergo sum.*[38] I am a responding being.

The dual nature of the self is found in its need for union and separation, interdependence and independence, community and society.[39] The dialectic of ethical reflection is generated by the tension between the moral context of community and the rational context of society. This is not to posit a dichotomy but a tension, for reason that seeks to be impartial and disinterested is still that of an embodied knower. Reason is not "pure" but cultural, historical, and human; it is "situated" reason. Moral authority is experienced initially within the community. The ethical stage of moral development is reached when communal authority is submitted to rational criticism. From socialization into and solidarity with a group, the person achieves individuation and aspires with universal intent to discern principles of justice and common good that embrace all groups and individuals on a basis of fairness and reciprocity.

Without individual and group conflict and crisis, ethics would not arise. Pluralism, conflict, and dissent are essential ingredients of democracy. Since conflicts are inevitable in an open society, education should give a central place to the consideration of conflicting values, differing moral arguments and levels of thought, and dilemmas of moral choice. The goal appropriate to both democracy and ethics is agreement on the principles of justice and the common good by which these conflicts can be resolved. Where rational agreement cannot be attained, respect for those of differing opinions and mutual assent to procedural rules for settling conflict are the basis for civil democratic society.

SUBJECTIVITY AND OBJECTIVITY

The second of the polarities in the dialectic of ethical thinking is the relation between subjectivity and objectivity. The task of ethics, traditionally viewed, is to prescribe behavior-governing principles of general validity. Since Kant, many moral philosophers have emphasized the universalizability of moral principles. They have been countered by positivists, who hold knowledge to consist exclusively of tautological propositions (mathematics and logic) and of objective, verifiable statements (science). In this view, ethics can be expressed only in emotive or subjective statements. The emotive theory of ethics accounts for moral discourse in terms of emotions, attitudes, or feelings of approval and disapproval. The grounds for objectivity in ethical reasoning are ruled out. Moral values and judgments are then solely subjective and arbitrary matters of taste, preference, and opinion. The alternative to the positivist view is not subjectivity but participation in cultural knowledge, which recognizes the less than wholly objective status of scientific knowledge and the more than simply subjective status of ethical judgment.

The emotive theory is a psychological account of meaning and, along with other versions of subjective individualism, denies a basis for common meaning to ethical terms. If judgments of value are only assertions of feeling and preference, and cannot be justified by reasons or rational argument, then ethical argument consists solely of suggestion or ordering. To affirm "That is good" is to say "I approve" (declarative) and/or "Do the same" (imperative). But our conception of "emotive meaning" is in fact determined "by some idea of how people *should* respond emotionally . . . and not simply by *every* emotional response that is in fact produced by the sign."[40] Analytic philosophers have not been content with emotivism for they have acknowledged the practice of philosophers of giving reasons.[41]

One's subjective feelings, both self-centered and other-regarding, can be objectified in rational reflection and evaluated along with those of others in the light of the total situation. The capacity of persons to transcend their appetites and interests and to consider them in the light of the needs and interests of others is limited but real. Moral language is often corrupted by its use in rationalization, propaganda, obscurantism, and moralistic posturing, but it testifies to the general belief that people can and should take into account the interests of others along with their own. Politicians often appeal to the love of country to justify questionable military ventures abroad. That kind of nationalistic chauvinism recognizes and exploits the moral impulse of citizens to sacrifice for others in time of need. Such moral feelings and values need to be subjected to critical examination. Ethics shares with all thought this critical function when it seeks to clarify and extend principles of judgment and to justify the choice of moral values and rules.

Objectivity in moral judgment is to be distinguished from objectivism. Objectivism posits knowledge that is impersonal, detached from the knower and independent of the creative context in which it emerges. It severs the relation between knower and known. It takes no account of the tacit knowledge on which all explicit knowledge depends. In contrast, the aim of objectivity in moral judgment is a comprehensive, accurate, and impartial assessment of the interests and needs of those affected by the decision. If the dialectical relation between subjectivity and objectivity is lost, personal responsibility for knowledge becomes equivocal. The psychologist Gregory Bateson expressed this forcefully, if colloquially, when he said: "My complaint with the kids I teach nowadays—graduate students and such—is that they don't really believe anything enough to get the tension between the data and the hypothesis. Whatever they may find out doesn't really impact on theory, because they don't have any theory; they're not willing to hold tight enough to get an impact. It *slides* all the time." [42]

The commitment of the knower to the truth one seeks, one's intellectual passions and reliance on the knowledge that one possesses but can never make wholly explicit, point up the importance for ethics of the conception of personal knowledge. Michael Polanyi declares that "this personal co-efficient, which shapes all factual knowledge, bridges in doing so the disjunction between subjectivity and objectivity. It implies the claim that man can transcend his own subjectivity by striving passionately to fulfil his personal obligations to universal standards." [43] If subjectivity and objectivity are seen as mutually opposed, knowledge will appear to be wholly objective and value purely subjective. In fact, however, knowledge and value are inseparable because they are bound to the knower in a community of persons who share responsibility for their knowledge.

TRADITION AND SITUATION

The third polarity of ethical reflection, the dialectic between tradition and situation, gives historical depth to the interplay between the individual and society. Morality is not the product of abstract reason but of social wisdom that develops over many years and is tested and revised in successive social settings. Tradition is often viewed as the antithesis of reason. Yet we continue to live off the capital of inherited ideas, social practices, ways of doing things, shared values and beliefs, usages into which we have been initiated and which constitute the cultural framework of society. Without respect for the authority of those traditions that have informed our intellectual and moral life, we undermine the foundations of our social existence. The moral framework of a society is the context for ethical reflection in changing situations. If this dialectic of tradition and situation is destroyed by a concept of reason that excludes its historical ground and tacit dimension, moral values are reduced to arbitrary assertions of taste and preference.

In stressing the importance of the dialectic between tradition and situation in ethics, we must again recognize the ascendance of rationalism in the modern period. The rationalistic spirit of the modern age was foreshadowed in Descartes's philosophic ideal of systematic doubt. When he set out to empty his mind of all inherited ideas and to rely upon clear and distinct ideas as the only knowledge worthy of the name—and then to describe his project in just such a clear, distinct, and lucid way—he delineated a model of knowing that has dominated the Western imagination ever since. The French Revolution itself represented a radical break with the past and the promise of a new age ushered in by unfettered reason and the power of man to manipulate and control his own destiny through self-conscious organization.

The rationalistic spirit was evident in the Founding Fathers of the American Republic, who were strongly influenced in their political thinking by John Locke and other rationalist thinkers of the Enlightenment. Historians have tended to see the Declaration of Independence as a product of the rationalist spirit. Michael Oakeshott has observed: "A civilization of pioneers is, almost unavoidably, a civilization of self-consciously self-made men, Rationalists by circumstance and not by reflection, who need no persuasion that knowledge begins with a *tabula rasa* and who regard the free mind, not even as the result of some artificial Cartesian purge, but as the gift of Almighty God, as Jefferson said."[44] But though the Americans were consciously critical of tradition and proud of their own unique creation, they achieved what they did not as rationalists contriving to design a constitution *de novo,* but as men schooled in the British tradition of liberty.[45]

Unless the historian's use of critical reason includes an appreciation for the traditional framework of thought, which is essentially tacit, it is destructive. Historical revisionism may debunk the pretensions, hypocrisies, myths, and ideologies of the past, but it also runs the risk of ignoring or rejecting those human values and traditions that help to generate its very criticism of the inhumanities of man. Tradition, like language, is the medium through which we attain the full reach of our critical powers. Michael Polanyi contends that "traditionalism, which requires us to believe before we know, and in order that we may know, is based on a deeper insight into the nature of knowledge and of the communication of knowledge than is a scientific rationalism that would permit us to believe only explicit statements based on tangible data and derived from these by a formal inference, open to repeated testing."[46]

The processes of creative renewal in the realms of science, law, and religion "always imply an appeal from a tradition as it *is* to a tradition as it *ought to be.*"[47] When the higher principles of mind and the intrinsic powers of our ideals are threatened by scientific reductionism or totalitarian control, we are challenged to examine the very foundations of a free society. These lie in an understanding of the person as knower and of an institutional framework that must be accepted as "the civic home of a free society."[48] In recognizing the character of the communal society we discover the grounds for a communal ethic.

We have formulated the ethical question as *What is my personal relation to what I know?* The question implies the dialectical relation between the situation of the knower and the moral and cultural tradition of which the knower is heir. Morality is rooted in the historical, concrete, and relative; ethics aspires to norms that are rational, objective, and universal. The dialectical process of ethical reflection moves between the two poles; a public ethic requires a communal base and a social context for critical reflection. The ideal of universality does not require the elimination of community traditions but the discovery of what is most central, vital, and enduring in them. In order to raise questions of social ethics with serious intent, we must presuppose a common political culture. The question is whether such a diverse and open society as our own does indeed have a communal morality. Tracing the dynamics of the dialectic of ethical reflection to the communal and societal nature of persons indicates a tentative and partial answer. We can go further by considering how this dialectic suggests regulative ideals for a social ethic.

The Search for a Social Ethic

A social ethic justified by a particular philosophical system is inevitably limited in appeal. Major philosophical systems have retained their vitality over long periods of time because they capture an aspect of truth that other systems fail to illuminate as well. But their assumptions, language, world-views, even their key notions, reflect the limitations of their historical settings.

The goal of the modern positivist was in part an effort to escape the relativity of history by sharply dividing factual statements from value claims. The price of this seeming resolution of the problem of the historical relativity of knowledge was a spurious claim of absolute objectivity for scientific statements and an unwarranted rejection of ethical statements as merely subjective expressions of taste and preference.

The common view that reduces ethics to the statement "It's up to the individual to choose for himself" reflects a climate of thought heavily influenced by positivism. The liberal version, "Individuals are free to do whatever they want as long as they don't harm anyone else," mirrors the assumption of positivism that ethics is an individual and private matter. These pervasive ideas about ethics can be traced in their philosophical lineage to David Hume and the dictum "You cannot derive an 'ought' from an 'is.'" G.E. Moore in the twentieth century seemed once and for all to discredit what he called the "naturalistic fallacy." Recently, Alasdair MacIntyre has cast an astringent eye on the whole field of ethics since the Enlightenment and found there a disaster area.[49] He contends that without a shared belief in an essential human nature (in the tradition of Aristotle), ethics dissolves. It would seem that the quest for a social ethic is doomed to futility.

Much of contemporary social theory affords no conceptual context for social ethics; its description of social "reality" makes social ideals seem unreal. But if moral community is acknowledged as a reality and incorporated in social theory, social ethics becomes a viable possibility. Its pursuit, then, depends not on a particular set of philosophical premises but on the recognition of the nature of social reality.

The moral-communal dimension of society is an abiding reality. We may employ the heuristic notion of the dialectical relation of community and society to explore the possibility of social ethics. This dialectical perspective reveals, negatively, crucial limitations in the two modern ethical traditions of utilitarianism and Kantianism and, positively, the theoretical and practical basis for the ethical ideals of justice and the common good.

UTILITARIANISM

As traditional concepts of morality began to lose their religious authority and were challenged by the new values of economic individualism, utilitarianism seemed to offer an objective ethical standard on which there could be public agreement. There were problems, however, which utilitarian social theory did not resolve. If, on the one hand, the good was viewed in terms of individual utility or happiness (pleasure, preference, the good as whatever one desires), the public good would be simply the sum total of individual goods, the greatest happiness of the greatest number. If, on the other hand, it was conceived in terms of specific projects for social reform, such as penal law, the moral concern for justice was cloaked in a "scientific" appeal based on what was in the general interest. This left unanswered, however, the question of how to account for the moral sense of obligation and justice; of how to measure happiness; or how, when there is a conflict between happiness and other values, such as justice, the conflict is to be resolved.

Utilitarian theory, based on the rational pursuit of one's own pleasure or happiness, must assume the moral obligation to seek the greatest happiness of the greatest number, but cannot explain or justify it. To be sure, one may seek the happiness of the greatest number if that is rationally perceived as contributing to one's own happiness. But what if an action might enhance only slightly one's own pleasure but cause harm to a large number of other people, or even only one other person? Could the utilitarian calculus of the social benefits of the Roman circus morally justify the sacrifice of the gladiator to the pleasure of the crowd? Utilitarianism fails to provide a satisfactory account of the moral obligation of the individual or a basis for the qualitative ethical evaluation of public policy.

KANT

In 1788, well before the peak period of utilitarianism's influence, Immanuel Kant in his *Critique of Practical Reason* mounted a formidable challenge to the utilitarian concept of nonmoral good, identified with pleasure. He gave a philosophical rendering of the Judeo-Christian concept of moral law, placing unconditional stress on the notion of obligation or duty. "We express two quite different judgments," Kant declared, "when we consider the *good* and *evil* of an action or the *weal* and *woe* . . . it brings."[50] The non-moral good is the object of one's natural desires for food, sex, health, companionship—in sum, happiness. But as rational beings, people distinguish between the nonmoral or natural goods conducive to their self-fulfillment and happiness and the moral good that they experience as obligation.[51] The Kantian tradition of deontological ethics insists on a fundamental distinction between science and morality that tends to disappear in utilitarianism, but it does so at the price of a bifurcation of inner and outer worlds.

Kant sought to establish the foundation of ethics in the rational individual so that ethics would be secure from the encroachment of empirical science. The result was a radical split between inner and outer worlds, the private and the public realms. The public world began to lose its meaning when it was confined to the development of more and more refined and efficient means, and ends were relegated to the private sphere. Ironically, Kant's thought can be seen as the greatest expression of *utilitarian* thought because his isolation of man as an end in himself removes meaningful ends from the public realm and reduces all of nature to means to his own ends.[52] With ends banished from the public realm and meaning restricted to utility, persons no longer shared a common world.

Utilitarian and Kantian ethics reflect the emerging individualism of modern society. While the categorical imperative stressed the universalizability of moral principles, it was, after all, a formal and hence empty principle. Kant was clear on what one should not do, lie, commit suicide and so on; he did not give guidance as to what one *should* do. The language of duties and obligations is part of a social vocabulary expressive of a way of life as a whole. If Kant's ethics seem abstract, formal, and empty to moderns, it reflects in part the fact that we can no longer assume the moral background of conventions and prejudgments that he and his readers could take for granted. Utilitarianism and Kantianism were both dependent for their rational cogency and moral appeal on a society that was still living on a substantial moral inheritance.

The social morality that Kant and the utilitarians could take for granted was changing as the growing economic system of capitalism made of the marketplace an arena in which individuals could by mutual consent treat one another as means to their own ends.[53] The social theory of capitalism and utilitarianism was an inadequate basis for social ethics because it restricted rationality to economic calculation and morality to private values. Without the recognition of the moral dimension of community, the social ideals of justice and the common good necessary for the continuing vitality of the civic society must appear sentimental and meaningless. Consistent with his view of community as a "fictitious entity," Jeremy Bentham gave short shrift to the idea of justice: "What happiness is, every man knows, because what pleasure is, every man knows, and what pain is, every man knows. But what justice is—this is what on every occasion is the subject-matter of dispute. Be the meaning of the word *justice* what it will, what regard is it entitled to otherwise than as a means to happiness."[54]

Justice

Justice has a solid grounding in political philosophy as a rational ideal, going back to Plato and Aristotle. It has survived the inroads of modern individualistic thought more successfully than the idea of the common good, which presupposes the reality of community. But while the concept of justice is congenial to modern thought because of the notion of equality entailed within it, its deepest significance cannot be perceived within an individualistic context. Justice and the legal order presuppose a moral community. We can speak of "an innate sense of justice" not as something inborn (a problematical and unnecessary idea) but as *intrinsic to our form of life as communal beings*. The sense of justice depends on a respect for others, a sympathetic identification with their point of view, a recognition of their claims on the community, and mutual responsibility for safeguarding the rights of the members of the community, all fostered in communal life.

The most widely discussed and influential treatment of justice by a contemporary philosopher, *The Theory of Justice* by John Rawls, takes the point of view of a prudential egoist situated behind a "veil of ignorance" and setting out to devise principles of justice for a society in which he might be randomly placed.[55] As a basis for hypothesizing general principles of fairness, the device is useful. In what would appear to be a position wholly antithetical to Rawls's contractarian view, Robert Nozick develops a laissez-faire approach to social justice.[56] Rawls and Nozick, however, in spite of their differences, share individualistic premises in their treatments of justice. Nevertheless, when Rawls turns to a discussion of the acquisition of the sense of justice, he does so in terms of the moral development of persons within a moral community.[57]

A communal view of justice is found in the ancient Greek philosophers. Plato and Aristotle are vulnerable to the criticisms that they confined their political theory to the city-state; limited their attention to the corporate unity of society to the neglect of the individual; and excluded women and slaves from the civic community.[58] But their enduring insight is that justice embraces the good of the whole community. In Aristotle's view it was men's sense of justice and their shared understanding of it that made a polis. Thomas Aquinas followed Aristotle in declaring that "every law is ordained to the common good."[59] Just as the modern development of capitalism and utilitarianism entails a reliance on community that is denied in theory, so the theories of justice in modern jurisprudence assume a communal value consensus that is ignored or denied in theory.[60] Since justice tends to be equated with legality in the modern period, it is important to examine the formalist and substantivist theories of justice.

The *formalist* sees law from a sociological perspective, as a system of rules developing over a period of time, the framework within which decisions are made about what ought to be done (the policy-making function of the legislature) and what has been done (the adjudicative function of the judiciary). For the formalist, whether positivist or analytical philosopher, the law is a given. There is no need or warrant to ask what it ought to be; the law is what the courts and legislative bodies say it is. This view goes back to Hobbes and Austin, who identified the law with the command of the sovereign, and is found in the modern school of legal realism.

The *substantivist* sees law from a moral perspective; the law reflects the continuing attempt to develop a consistent body of principles by which the ideal of justice can be applied in concrete decisions. The modern version of substantive law in the Western welfare-corporate states is "purposive law," in which law is designed to serve the purposes or policies of the state.[61] The problem for both formal and substantive law is that of the justification of the value standards by which the law is made and evaluated.

The authority of traditional morality is rejected by liberal thinkers such as John Stuart Mill, who confine law to a formal system of procedural rules. But the sanction for rules derives from the moral values and beliefs of the people. The authority of the legal system depends on the moral-communal dimension of legal justice; without it, authority must give way to power. Law is then experienced as coercion rather than as legitimate authority. The legal order depends for its justification on the moral (communal) order of society.[62] The explicit system of formal rules rests on the tacit acceptance of people. Ultimately the authority of legal justice depends on the recognition of substantive justice, the fairness and predictability of the content of the law. This is a question of shared values and common purpose of a society, absent in liberal legal theory because it is denied in principle as necessary or desirable.

The Common Good

It is not surprising that the notion of the common good today has been emptied of much of the meaning that it had for classical philosophers. The common good as equated with the utilitarian principle of the greatest good of the greatest number fails to include the good of those comparative few who are powerless, poor, and most needy. And if happiness is the goal, its definition will be elusive, for individuals' desires are varied and conflicting. If the common good is conceived as "the maximum fulfillment of all those aims that different men actually have, and the maximum satisfaction of their felt desires, whatever these may be, at the least cost,"[63] there is a problem of how to assess those often conflicting aims.

It is scarcely satisfactory, in Bentham's words, to "weight good against evil" by simply counting the interests of those involved, say, in the institution of slavery, from which some profit and others suffer. Some qualitative evaluation that distinguishes between desires and needs is necessary. If society is conceived exclusively as a collectivity of individuals, the common good, correspondingly, is the aggregation of individual interests. It can be determined simply and solely by quantifying the preferences, expressed interests, of those individuals. But qualitative evaluation of the common good is possible only if the society is also understood and experienced as a community of common purpose and shared values to which persons give their loyalty and affection. The social group is more than a collectivity, "a fictitious body," as Bentham called it; it has a reality and a meaning of its own. A communal point of view is necessary both for the just assessment of individual interests and needs and for qualitative evaluation of common values and goods.

The notion of the common good implies that community is a good in itself. Persons cooperate as well as compete, and they cooperate not merely for ulterior, self-seeking motives but because they enjoy the companionship and collaboration of their fellows. They care for other people; they can sympathize with the conditions, desires, and needs of others. They have a real, if limited, capacity for self-transcendence, altruism, benevolence, or love, as attested by religion, philosophy, social science, and personal experience. If community itself is a good, the determination of its concrete application in social policy should be a major concern in social ethics.

A proper concern for community and the common good, contrary to fears sometimes expressed by social theorists, will not lead inevitably to a totalitarian emphasis on the state as the supreme object of devotion. The opposite danger is more real in industrial "mass society"—the threat of totalitarianism arising out of the vacuum of community in which individuals are dependent only on the state and are vulnerable to its power and the economic forces unchecked by the state. Community at any level can become ingrown, intolerant, and exclusive. But insofar as community is essential to human development and fulfillment, it is a basic dimension of human nature and an inclusive ideal. Any particular human community is both a significant fact in itself and a symbol of the universal and inclusive human community.

A view of the common good that embraces the good of persons in community does not entail the sacrifice of the individual to community. Instead, it pertains to the conditions that make possible the fullest development of persons, the maximum expression of their powers and abilities. The common good is roughly synonymous with the "quality of life" of the community. It has to do with those goods that are indivisible—clean air, pleasant surroundings, public services, goods and amenities—and with the meaning of personal relationships, of work, and of one's place in the community, requirements of the good life residing in the functional and cultural interdependence of members of the community. The common good consists of goods that are meaningful because they are *shared;* we can only have them *together.*

The concept of the common good justifies some governmental measures that would be difficult to support on strictly individualistic grounds. In the controversy over flouridation, for example, some have argued that it employed mass medication and was a violation of private rights. In one case, the Illinois Supreme Court answered these charges with the argument that "even if considered to be medication in the true sense of the word, [flouridation] is so reasonably related to the common good that the right of the individual must give way."[64] The constitutional tradition upholding the regulatory power for health and safety is intended not merely to protect the rights of the private citizen but to promote the common good of the body politic.

The moral-communal dimension to our society provides the context for social ethics. As viewed in the abstract context of industrial society, the individual may appear to be without a communal context of meaning, value, and purpose. But viewed concretely, that same individual is a person formed in community, with a continuing network of personal relationships that enrich life and confer on it meaning and responsibilities. The idea of community, which has a precarious place in social theory, is vital to the lifeworld of persons. Against that background, we may inquire into the notion of the public realm.

3

THE PUBLIC REALM

I N TRYING to come to an ethical understanding of our relation to public life, we should distinguish between social ethics and public ethics. Social ethics represents the systematic effort to develop ethical principles applicable to society as a whole, drawing on theology or on the major philosophical traditions of natural law, deontology (Kant), and utilitarianism. Public ethics focuses more narrowly on the political or public realm and on the means of effecting change, specifically in policy making. Since the realm of the public is pluralistic, we shall not confine ourselves to a particular ethical tradition but engage in critical reflection on our common practices, institutions, and language usages, fastening on the ethical question as a way of exploring the nature of the citizen as public person.

The ethical question *What is my personal relation to what I know?* entails the question of value as well as of knowledge. In a pluralistic society with a diversity of communities and interest groups, value tends to be treated as private opinion even as knowledge is conceived as public. As knowledge is appropriated in the public world, it may appear to be impersonal and value free. This illusion grows, the farther the distance between myself and the public world. Knowledge seems to be more and more public and impersonal, value more and more private and personal. To the degree that societal habits of thought sanction this view of knowledge as value free, it will be impossible to hold public officials accountable for what they know. In that case, there is no basis for public ethics.

Some would welcome the disappearance of public ethics, in the belief that scientific knowledge and technological know-how are all that are needed to manage human affairs. But when knowledge is not applied on the basis of value choices open to critical debate by the political community, government becomes rule by experts. Likewise, when in the emotivist view value is relegated to the private sphere of taste and opinion, public life is deprived of standards by which citizens are to be treated as free and equal. Emotivism, observes Alasdair MacIntyre, "entails the obliteration of any genuine distinction between manipulative and nonmanipulative social relations."[1] The language of emotivism excludes any common standards by which to evaluate public behavior. When no one is to be held accountable for knowledge and value, the basis for public life dissolves.

The quest for a public ethic presupposes some idea of the public. We here explore the idea of the public as that realm in which, as free and equal citizens, we hold one another accountable for what we know in our common life. This idea can be considered against the background of notions of the public held by people in the West from the ancients to the present. It can help us discover more fully what we really believe about our public life and perhaps discern some possibilities that are excluded as long as some current notions of the public prevail.

The Idea of the Public

Modern ideas of the "public" have a shadowy background that can be traced to the ancient Greeks and Romans. In Aristotle's view, ethics was a branch of the study of politics and its prologue. The good life could be understood and attained only within the life of the city-state, the polis. Aristotle could not conceive of human life apart from the state, for "he who is unable to live in society, or who has no need because he is sufficient for himself, must be either a beast or a god."[2] Thus Aristotle was led to inquire into how the state should be organized in order to understand how the good of its citizens could be realized.

The public, for the ancient Greek, was distinguished from the sphere of the home and family life as the realm in which one presented oneself in political discourse and activity. While this corresponded roughly to our modern distinction between private and public, our view of the private has radically changed. Privacy for the Greek was, literally, privation; the idea of being confined to one's own (*idios*), was, literally, idiocy. Only much later in the eighteenth century did the concept of society, which is neither public nor private, come into use. For Plato and Aristotle, the social, the fact that men lived together, was not uniquely human but a condition shared by animals as well. It was the realm of the natural, of necessity, in contrast to the realm of the political, of freedom. To move from the household into the realm of the political was to act in such a way as to realize the uniquely human.[3]

The ancient Roman view of the *res publica,* the public ceremonies, military obligations, and ritual relations of citizens, became after the age of Augustus more and more formal and empty of civic passion. Richard Sennett observes that then, as now, public life became for most citizens a matter of formal obligation.[4] Just as the Romans finally imposed their private gods on the public world, so the modern privatized self psychologizes the public sphere as well. This projection of the psyche into the public order destroys the balance between public and private life, which in Sennett's view was achieved most notably in eighteenth-century Paris and London.

By the beginning of the eighteenth century, in English usage the adjective *public* had taken on a meaning similar to its meaning today: The public sphere was that in which one's actions were open to the gaze of others, in contrast to the private life of family and friends. During the Renaissance, the French used the word to refer mainly to the common good and the civil community. When the more modern term, *the public,* appeared in French around 1650, it had to do with the theatrical public, those in the court and city who were the audience for plays. By the eighteenth century, the *public* denoted the larger world of the cosmopolitan, in which one moved among strangers and acquaintances in the bustling intercourse of cafes, coffeeshops, inns, opera houses, theaters, and in promenades in the grand urban parks that were being built.

The inhabitant of the public realm of the eighteenth century was an actor, a performer. In his role (use of the masculine gender is intentional here—it was public *man*) he presented emotions comprehensible to his audience because they represented commonly understood experiences of social life. When the culture shifts from an interest in the representation of emotion to the individual's experience of it, the public man loses his social function and identity. Expression itself becomes privatized. At the same time, personality enters the public realm.

The balanced culture of public and private life that Sennett sees in the eighteenth century was disrupted with the rise of nineteenth-century capitalism. With the new secular worldview replacing the order of nature, nineteenth-century people began to look to personality as a way of finding meaning in the world.[5] Economic and social changes precipitated by the growth of industrial capitalism and large urban areas made it increasingly difficult to distinguish between classes and roles of those one encountered in public. Public man as actor had to be especially skilled to represent the feelings of others. And so, says Sennett, the identity of public man split into skilled performer and spectator. People began to judge politicians on the basis of their personalities and the credibility of their performance, just as they judged actors on the stage. Today, according to Sennett, the American electorate focuses on who the politician is rather than what he can do for them.[6] Fascination with the personality of the politician obscures the question of whether the politician is actually representing their real interests.

From the entrance of personality into the public realm in the nineteenth century to the "culture of narcissism" in our own time, preoccupation with personality, in Sennett's view, has drained the idea of the public of content and meaning. Seeing the public realm as impersonal and therefore valueless, people have only the family as a model for defining authentic relationships. An ideology of intimacy has developed in which "warmth is our god."[7] People look for community in which they can express their feelings and find a shared identity over against the larger, impersonal society.

Intimate community is not a model for political life. But there have been those from Aristotle to Jefferson and Tocqueville who have seen the small community as the home of civic virtue and the natural locus of fellowship and rational discussion. Does it make sense to conceive of complex, large-scale, heterogeneous industrial society as a political community?

The ideal of the political community has found expression from time to time in conservative reaction to liberal philosophy and industrial society, drawing inspiration in particular from Aristotle's polis or Jefferson's agrarian society. There has been a communal dimension to political practice and theory, even though very early in American history consumption became "the cement of the new system."[8]

This theme of community deserves more attention than it has received.[9] Though behavioral political scientists in the "realistic" tradition of Hobbes, such as Robert Dahl and David Easton, emphasize power rather than polis, political philosophers such as Hannah Arendt, Sheldon Wolin, Eric Voegelin, and Leo Strauss see the "political" as the sphere of the self-governing community in which citizens participate freely and responsibly. This "idealistic" concept of the political is at odds, however, with the view of politics most dominant in the American tradition of political philosophy, that of liberalism. The tension between self-interest and republican virtue is evident from the age of the Founding Fathers.

From Revolution to Constitution

As American freemen debated the form their government should take following the Declaration of Independence, the fear of an overbearing monarch was matched by a strong apprehension of the danger of democracy, equated by many with mob rule. A people made one by their struggle against the tyranny of government had been understandably cautious in refraining from delegating too much authority and power to a central government of their own. But men of property also needed safeguards against the unruly multitude of those governed by their passions. At least a very sizable number of the Founding Fathers saw it this way and insisted on writing into the Constitution stringent protections for the propertied. Between 1776 when the spirit of political liberty was at its peak and 1787 when the democratic revolution was crystallized in the writing of the Constitution, the direction of the American experiment was beginning to emerge.[10]

A comparison of the Declaration of Independence of 1776 with the Constitution of 1789 discloses a tension between political idealism and realism found also in varying degrees in the thought of the Founding Fathers and subsequent political thinkers.[11] The political discourse of 1776 had much to say about public virtue and the public good. The revolutionists invoked the phrase "the public good" almost as often as they did "liberty."[12] By 1789, the basic framework of the procedural state had been formed, an "American system of government" whose machinery was constructed to deal with the problem of factions and conflicts of interest.

Even in James Madison's thought, however, the majority's interest was not equated with the public interest. The historian Ralph Ketcham observes: "In a country where both the classical tradition and the Puritan Ethic were strong, Madison's stratagems for balancing power were not regarded as a means of *defining* the public interest (as his twentieth-century admirers of the 'conflict of interest' school of political science supposed) but rather as a way of *neutralizing* selfish factions so that a disinterested, virtuous public philosophy could be formulated and carried out."[13] Much more than token obeisance to the Puritan ethic is found in the political rhetoric of the day. John Adams, Benjamin Franklin, and Jefferson lay much stress on the virtues required of citizens by self-government. But the change of emphasis between 1776 and 1789 becomes more significant with the passing of time. The shift from concern in 1776 with the public good, republican ideals, and yeoman virtues to the constitutional proceduralism of 1789 would seem in retrospect to have foreclosed the likelihood of a continuing tradition of political philosophy and ethics. Some, in fact, have contended that America has lacked such a tradition from its beginning. It is true that American political theory has had a limited place for normative thought because it has stayed close to the realities of American political and economic life. Political theory has been throughout our history pragmatic both in the philosophical and "vulgar," or colloquial, sense of the word.[14]

It is inaccurate, however, to say that the thinkers of the revolutionary period were not serious and able political philosophers. They drew heavily on the liberal political philosophers, especially John Locke, but they applied philosophical abstractions to the concrete realities and unique situation of the nascent republic. The revolutionary leaders, declares Bernard Bailyn, were impelled by a spirit "at once quizzically pragmatic and loftily idealistic."[15] They were passionate pamphleteers, original in their emphases and use of the liberal theory of the time, and probing in their criticism of traditional concepts. Political debate included institutions that, like slavery, seemed to have little direct bearing on the struggle with England.[16]

If the revolutionary theorists were "pragmatic idealists," by the time the Constitution was signed the idealism had receded into the background. What remained was a sturdy, durable machinery of balanced powers and procedural rules in which government had the essentially negative role of guaranteeing order and the protection of individual rights. The safeguards

against bad government were such that they made good government difficult. The common purposes of a civic society inspired by the ideal of the
common good would presuppose a sense of community, and that was hardly
envisaged in a constitution that treated man as an atom of self-interest.[17]

The Fathers of Liberal Theory

The U.S. Constitution, like most of the state constitutions that preceded it,
gave primacy to economic individualism. The negative view of government was consonant with a negative view of the liberal ideals of reason
and freedom. Reason was instrumental, limited to the rational pursuit of
individual ends (within rules established by constitutional proceduralism).
Freedom was negatively viewed as the absence of governmental compul-
sion; its positive meaning was economic individualism.[18]

The conviction that economics is the chief concern of politics was
given classical expression in *The Federalist No. 10,* authored by Madison.
The rise of industrialism in the nineteenth century meant the end of the
Jeffersonian dream of an agrarian society of freeholders. There was a cen-
trifugal movement from settled society toward Western frontiers and a cen-
tripetal movement to city and factory. In this period of massive change, the
ideology of individualism preserved a sense of identity for the individual
and itself contributed to the processes of change separating the individual
from traditional authorities and the support of community institutions.[19]

From the age of Jackson, one may retrospectively glimpse the period
of creative formation of the ideals of American philosophy and life and
prospectively anticipate the developments of "liberal capitalism"[20] taking
shape in Jackson's time. The portentous significance for subsequent political history of developments in the Jacksonian age is suggested by a paradox
that Tocqueville made explicit with his formulation of individualism.[21] He
distinguished *individualism,* as the isolation of the individual, from *individuality,* which expressed itself in the political exercise of public virtue, in
company with others, to preserve liberty. The first was associated with
economic pursuit, the second with democratic ideals.

The tension between self-interested pursuit of private welfare and republican virtue in a free society threatened the equilibrium between Jef-

ferson's "formal image of a dynamic liberal society and the concrete image of a stable, virtuous yeoman republic."[22] Political leaders in the Jacksonian age struggled to reconcile republican and commercial values, "just as the two were splitting hopelessly apart."[23]

The persistent question in political theory of how a multitude of diverse private interests could be reconciled or harmoniously contained in a civic society seemed to many to find a solution in the combination of a self-regulating economy and the democratic system of constitutional checks and balances. Adam Smith had laid the foundation for the system in his *Wealth of Nations*. As individuals acting purely out of self-interest sought to increase their capital through saving and investment, they would unknowingly increase the capital of the whole, the division of labor, and the quantity and variety of goods on the market. The ideal behind Smith's theory was the same as that of nineteenth-century Social Darwinism: Men will progress, continually perfecting themselves and their society. The invisible hand of a flourishing American market economy was busily at work in the nineteenth century, opening up new frontiers of land, resources, and technology. Sanctified by the ideology of free enterprise and vindicated by tangible success on a grand scale, the invisible hand seemed indeed to be the hand of providence—far more beneficent than the visible hand of government.

The Pluralist Concept of Politics

Long after the appearance of the vast interlocking corporate structures of the modern American state, the capitalistic ideology of free enterprise was used to give a moralistic gloss to business practice. Capitalism as public philosophy, however, was replaced by the theory of pluralism.[24] It embraced the market economy and the political system in the optimistic view that both were self-regulating, together a machinery producing ever greater material benefits.

The theory of democratic pluralism, or more particularly interest-group pluralism,[25] was a response to the rise of industrial society and the problems it caused for classical democratic theory. In classical liberalism the citizen was related directly and immediately to the state. The emergence of mass politics and the displacement of family firms by large industrial corporations rendered that view obsolete. The citizen's relation to the state was now mediated through institutional associations. In addition to state and local governments and traditional voluntary associations, there were bureaucracies of government, business, and labor. Through the competition, bargaining, and accommodation of these interest groups, society was self-regulating, in this view.

According to modern pluralistic theory, a great number of political entities, including a hierarchy of municipal, state, and federal organizations and a wide variety of voluntary associations, affords citizens political expression and influence. In this view, conflicting interests and countervailing powers ensure that no particular group will be able to dominate the others. Government acts as a broker of interests; it sees to it that the rules are observed and the rights of individuals protected. Individuals exercise their political power through the vote (minimal in its actual effect) and through the political power of the groups with which they identify themselves.

Theorists of pluralism have attempted to adjust the democratic ideal to the realities of modern organizational life.[26] The result is a description of political life—or more aptly, the political system—as it "really is": government by interest groups, in which a productive economy and limited political participation by the citizenry ensure stability.

The preoccupation of liberal political theorists with the maintenance of stability leads them to shift their attention from the individual and the constitutional structures to the system, made up of economic actors. The system provides for the material well-being of the citizen. According to some of these pluralists, the functioning of the system may be disturbed, under certain conditions, by active political participation. Hence voter apathy is not necessarily bad but actually contributes to the stability of the system ("system maintenance").

In this view, decision making by political elites together with the apathy of the majority of the citizens ensures effective and harmonious working of the system. Procedural "rules of the game," tacitly accepted by the "players," make substantive democratic ideals unnecessary. When they become the subject of debate, they are a hindrance to the efficient working of the system.

In the theory of interest-group pluralism, informed moral choice by the citizen is not necessary and is not generally desirable. Neither are significant value choices possible or appropriate on the political level, since economic decisions are, and should be, made largely in the "private" sector. The citizen is dependent on the decisions made in the economic sphere of private bureaucracy; government bureaucracy itself intervenes only to assist in the process.

The Ethical Limitations of Pluralism

There are several limitations of pluralism, which derive from its parent tradition of liberal political theory, its view of American politics, and its behavioral methodology.

First, pluralism supports the status quo and favors those in power. Questions of justice are not likely to arise when the system is functioning in the way described, even though many are excluded from its benefits because they are not members of influential interest groups. The interests of minority groups, environmentalists, the handicapped, women, and many others have not been fairly represented.

Second, pluralism gives a restricted view of political reality. On the one hand, the theorists of interest-group pluralism, with their "value-free" methodology, reduce values and principles to interests, ignoring the moral-communal realities that sustain the civil community: mutual trust, shared values and concerns, confidence and loyalty, respect, honesty, and responsibility. The public interest in this view is not something to be debated and judged in terms of justice and the common good but is simply the outcome of the policy-making process. On the other hand, pluralists fail to take sufficient account of the way in which money, secrecy, and structural and procedural arrangements have protected those in power from competing interests.

Third, pluralism offers a truncated view of human nature. The ideal of human dignity and fulfillment in political activity in the pursuit of the common good is eclipsed by the model of the consumer of utilities motivated solely by self-interest. The liberal ideals of reason and freedom have been narrowed to economic rationality and economic opportunity.

Fourth, pluralism devalues democratic citizenship. It shifts attention from the citizen to the system. The citizen's rights and responsibilities may be accorded a formal place in constitutional theory, but, for pluralism, the ends of the system predominate over the ends of the citizen. Since political participation yields little satisfaction or "payoff," apathy is "rational" for the voter. Political apathy contributes to political stability. By definition, values contributing to the equilibrium of the system are identified as democratic.

Pluralism leaves private greed and public grabs unchallenged in theory and practice. It tenders no vision of a commonality of life transcending individual wants, nor of public purposes worth pursuing. If it is simply assumed that the way these interest groups operate is a natural and desirable expression of democracy, little will be done to improve the policy-making process. The societal perspective, however, views them in the light of their effects on society as a whole. John Gardner concludes: "The war of the parts against the whole is the central problem of pluralism today. We're moving toward a society so intricately organized that the working of the whole system may be halted if one part stops functioning. Thus our capacity to frustrate one another through non-cooperation has increased dramatically."[27] No community or society can survive, declares Gardner, without some subordination of group interests to the interest of the whole.

American democratic society prizes openness, variety, and tolerance. But it is more than a collectivity of atomistic individuals and interest groups. Its very existence as a state reflects a basic community of purpose. Pluralistic theory obscures the fact of the civil community and in so doing devalues civic virtue and public responsibility.

The Problematic Notion of Community

The theory of interest-group pluralism reflects the uncertain place of moral community in political theory, particularly that of liberalism. Liberal theorists developed the social contract theory in order to explain how men as autonomous individuals could live together in civil society. It is difficult, however, to see how self-interested and self-contained individuals could be induced to recognize the authority of civil community and restrain their self-interest out of a sense of obligation to the public interest.

The idea that individuals enter into a social contract because of rational self-interest ignores the fact that persons do not exist apart from society. By the time individuals come to political consciousness they have been shaped, along with their reason and their interests, by society. An adequate political theory will have to account for what we know of our own lifeworld, that we are creatures of community who have obligations to others that have to be considered along with our own interests.

Until the development of modern political theory, community was a central concept of political and legal philosophy. As Carl J. Friedrich has said: "From the well-known opening sentence of Aristotle's *Politics* to the French constitution of 1958, community has served to designate the human group with which politics and law are concerned and to which all the characteristic phenomena of political life, power, authority, law, and the rest must be referred."[28] Robert A. Nisbet calls community the "most fundamental and far-reaching of sociology's unit-ideas."[29]

The organic model of community was the fundamental form of social thought in classical anthropology.[30] Anthropologists have studied community in the round, since the locus of their inquiry typically has been a homogeneous group limited in size and complexity. Robert Redfield characterized folk society as a moral order, in contrast to the technical order of urban society. Primitive society is organized on a kin or tribal rather than political basis and is therefore a holistic and moral community. It is a world of person-to-person relations rather than a divided world of subjective self and objective other. Integrated man participates fully and directly in a whole range of cultural and technical activities. Art, religion, and daily life fuse in ritual drama that is both cathartic and creative, allowing primitive man to participate in cultural meanings that confirm his own sense of personal power and worth. The moral order is not a doctrine or something imposed upon a people; it is a way of life that is "always based on what is peculiarly human— sentiments, morality, conscience."[31]

Industrial society is the standard by which primitive society is often defined—and implicitly evaluated. For most of human history and for much of the world's people today, life has been lived in the village and small town. Only with the rise of modern industrialism has the primordial fact of small-scale human community become an artifact for Western urban people. In the complex life of contemporary America, with its emphasis on organization, technique, efficiency, and financial profit, community appears to be a relic of earlier and simpler ages. Some even see a time in the near future when the very meaning of *community* will be archaic and disappear from general usage.[32]

Individualism as a Form of Social Thought

A major factor responsible for the elusiveness of community in social theory can be traced to the pervasive power of a competing form of social thought—individualism.[33] With its origins in the thought of Hobbes, Locke, Hume, Adam Smith, and other Enlightenment thinkers, individualism as a root metaphor of social thought came to its most consistent expression in the utilitarianism of Jeremy Bentham, James Mill, and John Stuart Mill. The notion of the rational, free individual, generating his own wants and preferences, has been the fundamental tenet of classical liberalism. It is a dominant mode of political, economic, religious, ethical, and philosophical thought. This in spite of the fact that, in the words of George H. Mead, "a person is a personality because he belongs to a community, because he takes over the institutions of that community into his own conduct."[34]

In the liberal view of the political self, the citizen is motivated by interests to be pursued in the economic marketplace and in political competition. Since the individual knows his or her interests better than anyone else, the individual alone is entitled to define them. It follows that the individual can be viewed only in quantitative perspective, for as the utilitarian Jeremy Bentham put it, "Each one counts for one and only one." This may have the virtue of democratic numerical equality, but by ignoring any shared context of history and culture, it eliminates the basis for qualitative assessment and reasoned persuasion. The public interest cannot be defined, then, in normative terms of fundamental human needs and of basic requirements for a good society and a good life such as clean air, an aesthetic environment, public services and amenities. It is defined simply in terms of public preferences expressed in opinion polls and popular or representative votes. In the view of liberal individualism and pluralistic theory, values are treated as interests when they enter the economic and political spheres.

Individualism in America

The implications of individualism for public life in America were treated in the much discussed work of Robert Bellah and his associates in *Habits of the Heart*.[35] By the time it was published in 1985, a number of books dealing with the theme of community had appeared. None of them, however, captured the imagination of their readers as did the sociologist Robert Bellah and his three co-authors. Their highly readable critique of American culture generated extraordinary interest and discussion and became required reading in many college courses in political science, sociology, philosophy, and religion.

The enthusiastic reception given to *Habits of the Heart* by scholars and ordinary readers alike testifies to a widespread felt need. There has been a growing recognition of a "moral malaise" in American society. This malaise can be traced not only to disclosures of immorality in business, government, and professional life. A deeper source of unease is the sense that common moral standards have begun to disappear. It has become more and more difficult to talk publicly about moral obligations to other people and to the community. Selfishness has gained respectability with the term *self-interest,* while the language of commitment seems to become more and more foreign. The language of individualism is common to Americans, the language of community less congenial and less natural. But if moral language is to become a part of public discourse, Americans will have to rediscover the meaning of community.

The authors of *Habits of the Heart* conducted interviews with several hundred Americans in order to find out how they see their lives. They encouraged people to talk about what was most meaningful to them. These authors discern a common way of thinking and talking about marriage, work, church, politics, in spite of differences of sex, class, and work. This way of talking is peculiarly American, as a French visitor to America, Alexis de Tocqueville, noted over 150 years ago. It is the language of "individualism." That language allows individuals to express their interests and desires. It is limited, however, in giving voice to the moral obligations, relationships, and practices that actually characterize the lives of these people.

Brian Palmer, Margaret Oldham, and others who speak so well in the pages of *Habits of the Heart* are limited in their ability to make moral sense of the connectedness of their lives. These people are not "bad" or im-moral—they are, in fact, interesting and likable people—but they lack a language adequate to describe their moral experience. The moral language that comes naturally to them as Americans is called by the authors the "first language" of individualism. It is found in two forms, utilitarian individualism and expressive individualism.

Utilitarian individualism sees everything as a means to a self-interested goal, such as a career. Expressive individualism is concerned with "self-realization" or "self-actualization." It draws heavily on popular psychology or the "therapeutic" approach to personality and personal relations. It stresses the importance of "communication" but has little to say about commitments to others. The language of utilitarian and expressive individualism speaks in terms of the self's interests rather than the needs of others and of the common good. It reflects a lack of understanding of the essentially social or communal nature of the self.

The authors contend that if Americans are to make sense of their moral lives, they must draw on a "second language," the language of community. The language of community is the language of morality. It is the language of those who recognize bonds with others; it is necessary in order to speak of trust, care, love, commitment. While Americans think and speak largely in the first language of individualism, they grope for words to express their sense of shared responsibilities, social bonds, and common hopes that require the second language of community.

The language of community draws on two major traditions, biblical and civic, or "republican." The Judeo-Christian tradition keeps alive the meaning and experience of membership in a covenant community in which one is essentially related to others in trust and love and hope. The republican tradition goes back to ancient Greece and Rome, embodying the virtues and duties of the citizen. Both traditions stress the responsibility of the person to the common good of the community. This understanding of the responsible self is nurtured by communities of shared memory and hope, both religious and political communities.

The authors believe that the fragmentariness and loss of meaning in modern life can finally be healed only when people find ways to achieve a morally coherent view of life. That cannot come by returning to the community of the small town of the past. It might be possible, however, by reappropriating the cultural heritage kept alive in the biblical and republican traditions. The authors believe a transformation of American culture could result from social movements, such as the civil rights movement, which involve personal and social change and lead to greater political and economic justice. Private and public life are then fused in a meaningful way by commitments that link persons with the larger community in causes that transcend narrow self-interest.

The Debate over Community

Most critics of *Habits of the Heart* agree that the language of individualism is dominant in American life. Not all concur with the authors that the language of community is a viable alternative. It seems too reminiscent of the small town and too backward looking; it presupposes a sense of history that is lacking in Americans; it is inadequate for a large industrial society and for its future-oriented citizens. A number of critics find the language of the people interviewed to be less morally limited than do Bellah and his associates. They see greater moral agreement in American society than do the authors and perceive the diversity of moral traditions and practices in a more positive light.[36] A Marxist critic contends that the authors fail to recognize an alternative language to individualism, that of socialism, which America alone of Western industrialized nations refuses to include in its political and cultural discourse. A consequence of this is the inability to recognize the full extent to which capitalism shapes our private lives.[37]

How, then, are we to understand community in relation to public and private life? Whereas thinkers like Hannah Arendt saw private life expanding to displace traditional forms of the public in modern society, the authors of *Habits of the Heart* see the public sphere of economic relations encroaching on and becoming the model for personal life.[38] They urge the recovery of moral language by reestablishing connections with biblical and republican "communities of memory." Is this desirable? Is it even possible?

The nostalgia for small-scale community is misguided, in the view of Richard Sennett. As he sees it, the obsessive quest for intimacy and the psychological view of social reality robs society of civility. Sennett defines civility as "the activity which protects people from each other and yet allows them to enjoy each other's company. Wearing a mask is the essence of civility. Masks permit pure sociability, detached from the circumstances of power, malaise, and private feeling of those who wear them."[39] But community, in Sennett's view, is a false and destructive ideal: It is an ineffective means of political change, it consumes psychic energies better directed toward the pursuit of enlightened self-interest, and it easily becomes fratricidal.

The small community does present a problem for democracy, for the homogeneity of a like-minded group leads it to value social harmony, order, and stability above variety, dissent, and change. Informal patterns of dominant power relations are more difficult to challenge in small groups. The very impersonality of large groups encourages equality and a kind of liberty. Individuals have many different interests, which can best be expressed not in solidarity with one interest group but as members of a national constituency. Inclusive interests gain most support at the national level where leadership is responsible to the broadest constituency and so is likely to be concerned not with narrow but inclusive interests. The question remains, however, as to how self-interested individuals can be moved to seek the public good.

In Western political thought the polis has been the locus of democratic public life since the early Greeks and Romans. The conditions of metropolitan life in the great cities of the eighteenth and nineteenth centuries appeared to foster a convivial public life. In spite of changes taking place, Frederick Howe in 1905 could describe the industrial city as "the hope of democracy."[40]

The city brought together people of many different racial, ethnic, and economic backgrounds, knit them together in political organizations, provided newspapers and other means of communication and related them to city government and to each other. This rich public life was eroded with the further growth of cities, which has brought urban sprawl, economic segmentation, and life-style enclaves, with a consequent masking of diversity. Another reason for the deterioration of urban public life, according to the sociologist Craig Calhoun, is the fact that cities of 10 million are now absorbed into large-scale international economic systems and domestic political systems, creating a "mismatch between the urban scale of classical public life and the much larger scale of system integration in a world of indirect relationships and space-transcending technology."[41]

The city fostered public life as the space in which strangers could meet and converse and in which people could come to understand and appreciate human differences and the need to live together in civility. The very impersonality of the city contributed to this experience. To step into the public arena was to assume a social role. The desire for community and intimacy leads us to reject the public role and to demand that public figures be like ourselves. The preoccupation with public personalities rather than issues endangers public life. We need an understanding of the public in terms of something other than either the impersonality of the system world or the intimacy of the lifeworld.

Lifeworld and System World

Bellah's second language of community obscures significant differences between the realm of direct face-to-face relations and that of indirect relationships, which are mediated in society through large organizations, the mass media, and the market. The work of Jürgen Habermas is helpful in distinguishing between the two realms, which he designates lifeworld and system world.[42] The system world is the realm of state and market dominated by power and money; the lifeworld is one in which we talk with those we know about what is good and right, what we want to do, and how we can work together to achieve our purposes. Habermas finds a model for public discourse in the interpersonal relations of the lifeworld, in which communication is mutual, open, and free of distortion. He would extend that model of purified rational discourse to the arena of public discourse.

The view of interpersonal relations set forth by Habermas is an idealized one, of course, for power relations operate in the sphere of the lifeworld as well as that of the system world. Though they are not altogether separate spheres, lifeworld and system world should not be confused. On the one hand, the identification of the lifeworld of community with the system world of policy making leads to illusory solutions to political problems, as when President Reagan informed his television audience that balancing the federal budget was just like balancing the family check-book.[43] On the other hand, the complete separation of the lifeworld of community and the system world of large-scale society would seem to strip public life of qualities that make it human. The public sphere is not identical to, nor is it exclusive of, community.

Public life and the public good depend for their realization upon conditions distinct from the lifeworld of intimacy and from the system world of money and power. If public opinion is to be more than the sum of individual opinions, there must be a realm of public discourse in which citizens go beyond the expression of private opinions to consider those of other individuals, with a view to the possibility of changing their own. This entails a conception held by Habermas and others of the public sphere as a realm of discourse "interactively constituted by citizens and distinct from both state and economy."[44] How are we to conceive of the public as realm of discourse?

Public Discourse and Public Philosophy

Some would see the preservation of the public as dependent on a public philosophy. This assumes a community of citizens who reason together about the principles governing civic life. Such thinkers as the political commentator of a generation ago, Walter Lippmann, have believed that without some shared conception of natural law, of rational principles inherent in the very nature of things, the institutions of a free society would lack a basis of legitimacy. The American political temper, pragmatic, pluralistic, and secular, has not resonated to this theme. Walter Lippmann's *The Public Philosophy,* on which he had worked for sixteen years, was greeted in 1955 by disappointed and irritated reviewers who did not like his critique of popular sovereignty and the call for a stronger executive. Nor did they respond to the idea of a "higher law," the doctrine of a natural law "above the ruler and the sovereign people ... above the whole community of mortals." The reception was not surprising, for the notion of higher law was vague and its theological connotations bothered many of his readers. Lippman himself, says his biographer, was "a skeptic who yearned for an overvaulting sense of order he feared did not exist—the weakness that marred *The Public Philosophy*."[45] In his early notes for the book, written in the dark days preceding World War II, Lippmann had written, "Communism and Nazism are religions of proletarianized masses. ... A civilization must have a *religion*." But it was clear to many that a religious synthesis of culture was neither likely nor desirable.

A "public philosophy" understood as natural law presupposes a worldview whether of Roman stoicism or medieval Catholicism that no longer obtains in the modern world. Public philosophy should be conceived not as an official set of dogmas or moral absolutes but as a public forum. It represents not a "marketplace of ideas" but a mutual attempt by rational persons of goodwill to clarify and test moral principles by which policies should be judged. The search for absolutes on which general agreement could be reached, however, is both fruitless and unnecessary. We may find what we seek by reflecting on the way we have lived our lives, looking for those luminous ideas and ideals threaded through our history to which we have appealed in settling disputes, ordering our lives, and making corporate decisions. Members of a democratic society can arrive at approximations of justice and working definitions of "quality of life" through public debate and procedures designed to ensure broad participation in decision making. The key to this conception of the public is accountability.

The public may be defined as the space in which as citizens we hold one another accountable for what we know and value. Citizens are accountable to one another for the public good. Public good consists of what is necessary in order for persons to flourish, to have what they need to develop and expand their mental powers, skills, sensitivities, and moral imagination. To seek this is the aim of public ethics.

Public Ethics as the Creation of the Public

Morally serious conversation about the things that matter to us as human beings is what sustains a political community through the dissension and conflict that threaten its peace and even its existence at times. The best safeguard against such warfare is a continuing tradition of critical reflection on the institutions, practices, and projects of the society. This requires a community of citizens who take responsibility for what they know as moral beings. This personal moral knowledge provides a critical perspective on "official" knowledge controlled and manipulated by government, business, and the mass media.

Official knowledge is knowledge that is specialized, technical, and useful. Because of its seemingly objective character, we may forget that it is personal knowledge, validated by our general knowledge and our values. But as it is absorbed and integrated into the system world, its connection with our personal experience, with the lifeworld, may be obscured. Official knowledge will seem to be objective, impersonal, verifiable—*public,* whereas moral knowledge will seem to be subjective, unverifiable, and private. When this split between knowledge and value is maintained, no effective challenge to official knowledge is possible, nor is there any leverage for a critical moral perspective on public policy making. Official knowledge becomes the property of a ruling elite, whether government or business. To understand knowledge as public rather than official, however, renders politician, technocrat, and bureaucrat accountable to the citizenry for their decisions and for the process of decision making itself. Public knowledge implies as well the responsibility of the citizenry in participating in collective decision making. This makes official knowledge a matter of public ethics.

Public ethics as an academic project embodies and makes concrete the kind of public conversation that can humanize policy making. By its nature it is interdisciplinary, bringing together different professional, scientific, and political points of view to focus on particular policy issues with a view to arriving at wise, just, and humane decisions. It provides a model for public discourse. Considerations of money and power affect policy proposals far less here than in the political and business worlds.

Public ethics as a discipline is paradigmatic of public discourse. It utilizes a variously skilled intellectual community to analyze and evaluate public issues. But it is not the responsibility of trained professionals alone. The citizen's responsibility extends beyond the vote in elections by which the state is held accountable to the electorate. The citizen is accountable to others for the critical perspective on state policy that his or her knowledge

and value commitments provide. A primary responsibility is the integrity
of the language of public speech itself.

The Perversion of Public Speech

Language appropriate to public ethics is rich in nuance, dependent for
meaning on social context and a cultural tradition of discourse. When persons do not hold hold themselves accountable to community, language
loses the connection with the lifeworld and is reduced to the quantifiable,
the objectifiable, the mechanical. It has less to do with social reality and
more to do with the manipulation of images. The purpose of language is
then not to express truth but to sell something, whether toothpaste or
president. In *The Selling of the President,* Joe McGinnis gave a full-scale case
study of this process. It was pithily summarized in a memo by Richard
Nixon's adviser Ray Price in which he set forth the strategy aimed at
overcoming the public's view of Richard Nixon. They would advertise
the "new Nixon" as a man that had grown and matured. Never mind
about the reality of Nixon the man: "*We have to be very clear on this point:
that the response is to the image, not to the man. . . .* It's not what's *there* that
counts, it's what's projected—and, carrying it one step further, it's not
what *he* projects but rather what the voter receives. It's not the man we
have to change, but rather the *received impression.* And this impression often
depends more on the medium and its use than it does on the candidate
himself." [46] If the memo no longer has the capacity to surprise or dismay,
it is because subsequent presidential campaigns have simply elaborated the
advertising techniques employed by the Nixon media experts.

If language is used to distort the reality of the man on the way to the
presidential office, once he is there it may be used to protect his interests
and deflect public scrutiny of government operations. When President
Nixon's press secretary Ron Ziegler was asked about earlier statements
that were discovered to be false, he did not admit that they were lies but
simply declared them to be "inoperative." Official language cannot be
trusted because it is tailored to the interests of government. Public speech,
in contrast to official language, is oriented to the public interest and directed to real persons, who can be expected to respond with intelligence

and feeling. It is reciprocal language rather than one-way, top-down language of official government and bureaucracy. It is conversation among free and equal citizens.

Public Speech versus Bureaucratic Language

The citizen who would hold public officials accountable must be aware of the nature of bureaucratic language. It is a very specialized language, restricted to rules laid down from above and allowing little discretion to the bureaucrat. The aim is not mutual understanding on the basis of communication but the transmission of information from above to be accepted and obeyed. Social relations are converted into control relations. Persons are turned into clients, to be treated on the basis of bureaucratic rules rather than the person's individual needs. The client becomes the victim of a language barrier, as illustrated in the story of Pasquale Plescia, a man who traveled from California to Washington, D.C., to try to solve the problem of the delays in his social security checks:

> "Well, I'll tell you something about this town. They got a secret language here. You know that? Bureaucratese. Same thing we used to call double-talk. These government people, they don't hear you. They don't listen. You start to say something and they shut you out mentally, figuring they know right away what you're going to say before you say it.
>
> "I knocked on doors here for two weeks but everyone's so busy with paperwork, they got no time for nothing else. I go to see one Congressman—a priest, so I figure he's got humanitarian interests—and his aide says I got to write him a letter first. Another one won't let me in cause I'm not in his constituency. Another gives me a press release and says, 'This is the Congressman's position on Social Security.' No kidding, that happened. So I go down to HEW. They've got 180,000 people working for HEW, and you know what? They've got nobody to make a complaint to."[47]

The language of bureaucracy, like that of computer "language," consists of fragments of information received as instructions, not knowledge to be comprehended by reasoning. Computers do not think, nor, insofar as they simply follow the rules, do bureaucrats. Programmed thinking has the yes–no character of computer language and is incapable of perceiving gradations of quality and distinctions of meaning dependent for their understanding on knowledge of the lifeworld. To understand and evaluate information one must exercise qualitative judgment. All the bureaucrat has to do is go by the book. But when we engage in genuine public speech we have to think for ourselves, weighing the issue in the light of what we know and holding ourselves accountable to others for the truth. If the question for the bureaucrat is What does it say in the rule book? the question for us when we hold ourselves accountable to others is *What is my personal relation to what I know?*

When people speak as functionaries they have no personal relation to what they say other than how it may affect their position, power, or profit. Wendell Berry, who is a farmer, writer, and professor of English, has dissected the language of officialese with a sharp eye to the ways in which it severs connection with the social world of meaning and experience. He sees this in the official reaction to the crisis of the Three Mile Island nuclear plant breakdown. Members of the Nuclear Regulatory Commission tried to devise a press release that would reassure a fearful public. When a commissioner suggested that the statement should indicate the possibility of a meltdown, Commissioner Kennedy said: "Well I understand what you're saying. . . . You could put a little sentence in right there . . . to say, were this—in the unlikely event that this occurred, increased temperatures would result and possible further fuel damage."[48] The commissioners absented themselves as human beings and turned a public danger into a technical problem. Berry concludes: "Public responsibility becomes public relations, apparently, for want of a language adequately responsive to its subject."[49]

In another essay, Berry recalls a meeting he attended in which representatives of Public Service Indiana tried to reassure assembled citizens of local communities that the nuclear power plant being built at Marble Hill posed no danger.[50] The fears and questions of the citizens were met with

technical jargon and bland assurances until a woman rose from the audience to ask the group of officials a question: How many of you live within
the 50-mile danger zone around Marble Hill? The startled men on the
stage had to answer, Not one. Berry sees here one example of a deepening
division in the country between citizens who are trying to protect their life
in community and officials who come from a safe distant place to pacify
citizens with the jargon of expertise, protected by their professional roles
and untouched by the values of home and community.

Standing by Our Words

We bind ourselves to one another and to reality by words. We need words
to nourish and keep alive all the things we cherish most, love and loyalty,
beauty and imagination, work and play, truth and trust. Faith itself is dependent on words that point beyond themselves to what cannot be captured in words. When words are used to deceive or to confuse, when the
speaker does not mean what he or she says, our sense of reality is threatened. We become uneasy when we find ourselves in a foreign country
where all around us are speaking a strange language. Before long, we are
likely to feel disengaged from ourselves as well as our surroundings. We
long for home and return there as soon as we can. But when in our own
native land we hear familiar language that begins to betray a loss of connection with the realities it signifies, we have no place to go. Our home,
our sense of place, our location and connections, our very identity are at
peril.

The danger is that we will not realize what we have lost. We begin
to take the language of advertising and officialese for granted. There is
little public outrage when it is disclosed that a president has lied to cover
up an invasion of Cambodia or another has negotiated secret arms deals
with Iran or that *contra* forces in Central America were illegally funded.
Lies become "disinformation." The "wordfact" of George Orwell's *1984*
threatens to become the staple of public relations in business and government.

Our hope for a free and democratic society and for the integrity of
our own lives lies in our willingness to stand behind our words. The coun-

terpoint to the empty language of officialese is the words spoken by citizens who back them with their lives. The Freedom Riders of the civil rights movement and those who protested the Vietnam war discovered the weight of their words. So did one white middle-class woman, Erica Bouza, the wife of the police chief of Minneapolis, whose arrest was widely reported after she began to take part in peace demonstrations. She said:

> "You get to a certain point in your life and you have to pay back. You have to do something in return. Because I'm a citizen and I have freedom of speech, I have to utilize these things. If I'm critical of my country, I do it in the same way that I'm critical of my children. I want to make it better and stronger. Where I'm not happy with what is happening, I have to speak up. I don't think being a citizen is just standing up and singing the national anthem or saying the pledge of allegiance. It's being informed and speaking out. I believe each human being can change the world a little bit. If you do nothing, nothing will change."[51]

Mrs. Bouza said that, following her arrest, she was asked to speak. When she found that people were listening to her, she said she became much more aware and began to read and learn as much as she could. When words are taken seriously, citizenship assumes new meaning.

Lifeworld and Public Policy

To hold each other accountable for what we know is to take a critical-constructive perspective on institutions based on our lifeworld of experience, knowledge, and value. If the public consists only of the system world, knowledge will be treated as something impersonal, quantitative and value free. The paradigm for knowledge will be scientific, "hard," masculine, in contrast to moral knowledge, seen as subjective, expressive, and feminine. The public world will be drained of those qualities that give texture, color, warmth, sound to our lives. Public policy making becomes an abstracted exercise when it is not sensitive and open to the lifeworld.

What is missing in much public policy, and even more in theories about public policy, is the knowledge and experience of the day-to-day world inhabited by ordinary people. Some feminists are calling attention to the "powers of the weak" that are largely ignored in official views of the world: the ability to cope with problems that require practical know-how and resourcefulness; the recognition of one's vulnerability and dependence on others; sensitivity to others' feelings and points of view; nurturing skills and pleasure in helping others, especially the young; independence of judgment based on one's situation and not bound to the status quo. The "outside-the-conventional-framework knowledge" that Elizabeth Janeway sees as the possession of women and other minorities is precisely the knowledge most needed in dealing with public problems of poverty, racism, and war.[52] The world holds together and life goes on because of the competence, creativity, care, and hard work of the "weak." Their tacit knowledge underlies the rational considerations made explicit in public policy. But it needs to play a more determinative role in the policy-making process.

When knowledge of the lifeworld is ignored, policy suffers. Federal emergency relief was provided in the aftermath of the flood disaster at Buffalo Creek, West Virginia, in February 1972. When the dam gave way, it sent a torrent of sludge-filled water through the narrow mountain hollow, killing 125 people and destroying the mining village. The U.S. Department of Housing and Urban Development (HUD) went to work quickly, supplying aid to the victims. Relief efforts were well meant. But the aid was administered without concern for the community life of the inhabitants, who were assigned to trailer camps without regard to kinship or neighborhood ties. Officials placed people in the temporary housing as quickly as possible, but those 2500 persons lived in trailer camps for longer than a year. Devastated by their individual traumas of confusion, despair, and hopelessness, they experienced also the collective trauma of what sociologist Kai T. Erikson calls the "loss of communality."[53]

The result was depression, apathy, and demoralization. There was a severe sense of disorientation, moral disintegration, a loss of connection with spouses and friends, increased illness, and a haunting fear.

In his study of the effects of the flood disaster on the people involved, Erikson is led to reflect on what the loss of community means not only to the members of the mountain village of Buffalo Creek, West Virginia, but to the rest of us as well. Traumas, he observes, can be induced by chronic conditions as well as acute events. Erikson wonders whether traumatization is likely to become more and more common as a result of separation from the nourishing roots of community. His conclusion can serve as a caution and reminder to policy makers: "What happened on Buffalo Creek, then, can serve as a reminder that the preservation (or restoration) of communal forms of life must become a lasting concern, not only for those charged with healing the wounds of acute disaster but for those charged with planning a truly human future."[54]

The relevance of the lifeworld perspective to policy making can be seen in federal policy on urban renewal in the 1960s and early 1970s. Large areas of poor neighborhoods were razed to the ground and replaced with high-rise apartments and other kinds of modern but mass-produced housing, which resulted in sterile surroundings. Insofar as slum-clearance projects were intended to improve the lot of the poor, they failed from the point of view of the tenants themselves. Modern facilities could not make up for the sense of devastation tenants felt because of being uprooted from their homes. Urban renewal policy, well-intentioned though it was, reflected a lack of sensitivity to the community ties, the independence, dignity, and pride possessed by people who had a strong sense of place and neighborhood spirit even though poor. The speedy deterioration of the large housing complexes in the inner cities testified to the loss of the communal spirit of the inhabitants. A notion of the public interest was imposed from above by the experts, rather than perceived in terms of the lifeworld of the people affected by the policy.

The Public Interest and the Public

In pluralist theory the notion of the public interest loses its connection with the public as a whole. It has nothing to do with ideas about the common good to be debated and decided in the public sphere. In the pluralist view the public interest is simply what emerges from the competition of interest groups. The public manager's task was intermediation among interest groups. In addition to this procedural vision of public administration was the view of maximizing net benefits.[55] As intermediator between conflicting interests, the public manager was referee; as net benefit maximizer, the administrator was analyst, using the tools of cost-benefit analysis and microeconomic theory to improve overall economic efficiency. Both of these views shared the pluralist assumption that the public interest was to be defined by the selfish preferences of individuals. The public itself was dissolved into private interests.

The two views of public interest fail to take into account the ways in which the very procedures used in policy making influence people's views of their interests and values. "The official act of placing a monetary value on the upstream wilderness," says Robert Reich, "constitutes a powerful public statement that feelings toward such wilderness *can* be expressed in monetary terms."[56] It transforms something valuable in itself and treasured by the whole community into a market commodity and evaluates it on the basis of "willingness to pay" to travel there. This ignores the fact that many value the wilderness area for itself, simply because it exists. But the official policy creates social norms that affect the way citizens will think about the environment in the future.

When the public is included in the policy-making process not simply as individuals seeking their disparate interests but as participants in deliberation about what is good for society, new possibilities emerge. As citizens share information and ideas, they may come to see an issue differently. They may volunteer time and money as they see others participating in community projects. They may decide that the community good deserves priority over their pecuniary interests. In contrast with policy making based on interest-group intermediation and net benefit maximization, public deliberation allows people to discuss ideas, discover shared values, and recognize deeper conflicts that need to be confronted and resolved. The public interest is then more than neutral, procedural policy making. It is deliberation by citizens about public values.

If citizens are not able or willing to think about these matters and to hold their political representatives responsible for informed moral judgment about them, decision making will be left to a few people in strategic positions. Their power will grow in direct proportion to the degree of secrecy cloaking their decisions. It will not be the power to act for the good of all, however, but for their own benefit. Unchecked by reference to moral norms or popular will, power will tend to be exploited for private purposes. Public issues call for a communal lifeworld perspective, both to understand the issues in their proper context and to respond to them as matters affecting the well-being of the whole community. To leave our corporate fate to a self-interested elite of specialists and politicians is to forfeit our responsibilities of citizenship and make way for an authoritarian government. Liberalism's equation of values with interests and its identification of interest-group pluralism with democratic policy making leaves no basis for raising the ethical question. But the issues facing us require ethical judgment; that in turn depends on public morality, a commitment to public values transcending narrow self-interest. To hold ourselves accountable to others for what we know and say and do is to create the public.

Conclusion

Public discourse that holds officials accountable to human needs and the public good requires a citizenry that can reason together. There is disturbing evidence that public schools in America are failing to educate people to think. In a 1989 report, the National Assessment of Educational Progress evaluated the progress of students over the past twenty years.[57] While it found that basic reading, writing, math, and science skills had improved, the study revealed that few students could apply them in ways that would help them in college, on the job, or in daily life. "We have a solid foundation of basic skills," said the report, but "there is stagnation as far as high-order thinking skills are concerned." It urged that teachers redesign curriculum and tests in order to get students to analyze what they know, rather than just learn facts and rules.

An essential feature of public discourse was highlighted in an undergraduate class discussion several years ago, which was conducted by the professor and observed by his colleagues during a faculty retreat. At the conclusion of a thoughtful and spirited conversation, a faculty member asked the students, "What difference would it have made if your professor had not been present?" The silence suggested that the students were having difficulty answering the question. Finally, one of them said, "His presence was essential. Otherwise it would have been a bull session. He holds us accountable for what we say." The commitment to make ourselves accountable for what we know links the university as a community of learning with the civic world in a shared search for the good. In the public realm those aspects of person and position, of status and role, that separate us and render us unequal in the private realm are irrelevant. We speak to each other as equals. The moral understanding of ourselves as citizens requires that we know who we are as free and equal citizens.

4

CHOOSING WHO WE ARE

I
N ASKING the ethical question *What is my personal relation to what I know?* I am asking, Who am I? My self-identity is a function of my relationship with others, not of private knowledge but of interpersonal relations that give texture and pattern and substance to the concept of self. I am initiated into a community of knowers. My knowledge is bound up with my identity as a member of the community. I am responsible for what I know and, in my public life, accountable to others for what I know.

We are accountable to one another in the public realm for what we know and value as free and equal citizens. Our understanding of ourselves as citizens, our self-identity, is shaped by the values in our American moral tradition. We have but to recall the words of the Declaration of Independence to recognize the essential tie between the values affirmed there and our own self-identity as Americans: "We hold these truths to be self-evident, that all men are created equal; that they are endowed by their Creator with certain unalienable rights; that among these are life, liberty, and the pursuit of happiness." These words are at the heart of the distinctive value system transmitted by a people from generation to generation. It is what social scientists call *political culture*. Deeply held cultural values are more crucial to a political system than the opinions on daily matters of public policy collected in public opinion polls.[1] As the communal value system, culture is, in the broadest sense, the morality of a society. Political culture forms our understanding of who we are as citizens.

From time to time, Americans have found it necessary to reflect critically on their self-identity as a people. The Civil War was such an historical moment. So were the Populist and Progressive responses to the excesses of industrialism; governmental action in the Great Depression; the civil rights struggle; and the conflict over the Vietnam war. These times of national crisis provoked many to come to a deeper and more inclusive understanding of themselves and their society. If today we are to become a more inclusive community, we may have to reexamine our traditional values. That everybody in the society does not count equally, for example, may in part reflect the way Americans have conceived of the values of liberty, equality, property, and religion.

Core Values in the American Liberal Tradition

The continuity and distinctive features that most historians and cultural critics find in the core American values derive from the liberal tradition. *Liberalism* is an elusive term to define because of its changing connotations over the past several centuries. It is best to follow Louis Hartz and others who see liberalism as the broad political tradition that includes both liberal and conservative in the popular use of the terms.[2] A historical value consensus can be traced back to its roots in the thought of John Locke, the philosopher of the English Enlightenment who was the most influential spokesman for liberal philosophy. The earliest colonists to America brought with them this liberal value tradition, which was adapted to American conditions and incorporated in the Constitution by James Madison and other Founding Fathers. While the contributions of Puritanism to democracy were more significant than is often acknowledged,[3] the Constitution reflects the strong influence of the liberal tradition.

American liberalism was a fusion of, first, the classical political ideals of freedom and reason the colonists brought with them and expressed in the Declaration of Independence and, second, the aspirations of economic individualism embodied in the constitutional protection of private property. For Locke, private property was the bulwark of liberty. Only freeholders with economic independence could maintain their political freedom. In Locke's theory, the government's sole purpose was to protect men from each other, to preserve life, liberty, and property. Constitutional

government, safeguarded by effective restraints, became the institutionalized expression of liberalism.

The core values in the American liberal tradition are liberty, equality,
property, and religion. These values, associated with the tradition of political thought going back to John Locke, find strong agreement among a
large number of writers on American values and beliefs and are widely
supported, according to opinion polls taken between 1935 and 1970.[4] They
were perceptively described in the 1830s by a French visitor to America,
Alexis de Tocqueville. These values, he asserted, could be understood in
terms of a unifying principle of democracy that was both a political and a
social ideal: "equality of condition."

Tocqueville no doubt overestimated the extent and degree of equality
in America, but he was most impressed with what the principle of equality
portended for the future. Tocqueville was filled with a kind of religious
awe as he contemplated the inexorable course of the leveling process of
equality that eliminated traditional authority, reduced all men to the same
moral and intellectual dimensions, isolated each, and made a benevolent ty-
rant of the public. "Thus, not only does democracy make every man forget
his ancestors," he declared, "but it hides his descendants and separates his
contemporaries from him; it throws him back forever upon himself alone,
and threatens in the end to confine him entirely within the solitude of his
own heart."[5] Tocqueville characterized the personality type that he saw
produced by equality of condition by the word "individualism." Whereas
individuality was a robust term applicable to the democratic citizen and expressed in public virtue, *individualism* connoted preoccupation with self-interest and economic pursuit. The democratic ideals of the revolutionary age
and the developments of liberal capitalism were increasingly at odds when
Tocqueville visited America, during Andrew Jackson's presidency.

The notion of "rugged individualism" at the heart of free enterprise
ideology grew under the challenge of the frontier. The natural conditions
of the New World, inlcuding geographical, profoundly influenced Americans in the development of their social, political, and economic institutions
and in their self-image, though David Potter has persuasively argued that it
was not the frontier as such that was the decisive factor in the development
of the American character but the fact of abundance in its various forms.[6]

Religion and Property

The history of early American Puritanism reveals a most striking fact: While ministers denounced the conduct of tradesmen and laborers, they never condemned trade or laboring. To work hard in one's calling was the will of God. In describing the Protestant ethic, Perry Miller said that for the Puritans, a right to property, "exercised within civil propriety, is as valid for the pagan or idolater as for the saint."[7] The combination of free enterprise ideology and a secularized Protestant ethic became a driving force in American life (however much historians may debate the role of Protestantism in the rise of European capitalism).[8] Weber saw Benjamin Franklin as the exemplar of the gospel of work. After a long and distinguished public career, Franklin would leave a will beginning with the words "I, Benjamin Franklin, Printer." An easy self-justification in the pursuit of wealth enabled Americans to ignore, deny, or excuse the results of their pursuit of what were felt to be justifiable ends. Possession of property was not only nine-tenths of the law, it was palpable evidence of superior character, the just and natural reward for the virtues of the possessor.

This complex of economic and moral ideas was further affected toward the end of the last century by the impact of Darwinian thought in America. Social Darwinism applied the theory of biological evolution to society.[9] The ideas of natural selection, of the struggle for existence, and "survival of the fittest" were taken to mean that the winners in the competitive struggle were thereby demonstrated to be superior. It followed that whatever interfered with this struggle was a hindrance to the evolution of the human race. Social Darwinism reinforced the Protestant ethic in its emphasis on the value of hard work, unremitting struggle, competition, and achievement. The vices of laziness and indolence would be punished by poverty, hunger, and want.

The democratic ideal of American society, the secularized Protestant ethic, the frontier, and free enterprise fostered a unique American character. The principle of individualism, in which the universal ideals of liberty and equality were implicit, gave a national identity to American society. With the growth of nationalism in the nineteenth century and the crisis of the Civil War, the American way of life came more and more to be defined by individualism. It became an ideology that gave unity, continuity, and purpose to a heterogeneous people. Seeming to explain all that was distinctive and best about the country, it shared the universal and messianic character of socialism while preventing it from ever becoming a viable political option in America. Individualism wedded with nationalism became synonymous with Americanism.[10] The core American values of equality, liberty, property, and religion are largely defined and delimited in terms of individualism. We should note, however, the *moral* element in the individualistic understanding of religion and property. This is illustrated in the treatment of the Native American, the American Indian.

The American Indian

In 1887 an issue of public policy that had long agitated white Americans was settled. The Dawes Act was passed, fixing federal policy toward the American Indian for the next forty years. The policy was based on the assumption that Indians should ultimately be incorporated into American society as farmers and citizens. Well-intentioned religious leaders had joined with legislators in arguing for the civilizing of the Indian through abolition of the tribal system and the introduction of private property.

The way for Indians to prepare to become individual citizens, according to pronouncements from some leading pulpits, was by hard work, individual responsibility, acquisition of property, and family life. President Merrill E. Gates of Rutgers College declared: "There is no other 'manifest destiny' for any man. . . . To this we stand committed, by all the logic of two thousand years of Teutonic and Anglo-Saxon history, since Arminius . . . made a stand for liberty against the legions of Rome." Tribal organization had to be broken up because community of land and goods "cuts the nerve of all that manful effort which political economy teaches us proceeds from the desire for wealth." Senator Dawes agreed with Gates that "the desire for the acquisition of property is . . . on the whole the mainspring that daily keeps in motion the mechanism of the world's daily routine."[11]

The Dawes Act illustrates the way in which values of the political culture shape the policy-making process. The political situation in which the Dawes Act was passed was interpreted through the value screen of the Protestant work ethic and the notions of progress and survival of the fittest, current in the popular philosophy of Herbert Spencer. The Dawes Act destroyed the Indians' communal way of life, denied their historical identity, and opposed their values of tribe and nature in the name of liberty, individualism, property, and religion.

Ironically, the Indians' way of life more closely approximated the early American ideal than any of the cultures white settlers established. As the historian Gary Nash observed about colonial America: "Many of the early colonists had envisioned a virtuous society organized around concepts of 'reciprocity, spirituality and community.' With the passage of time and with the steady growth of the white population, however, 'the only people in North America who were upholding these values, and organizing their society around them, were the people who were being driven from the land.' "[12] It would be difficult to find an event that more graphically reflects the moral ethos in nineteenth-century America than the Dawes Act of 1887. If religion and property were so understood in the American value tradition, how were liberty and equality understood?

Liberty and Equality

In the revolutionary era, "liberty" was the overriding theme of political discourse. For late-eighteenth-century Americans, "equal liberty," as it was everywhere referred to, meant freedom from government oppression.[13] It meant the freedom of Americans to be let alone to control their own lives. Americans believed, with John Locke, that private ownership of property was the best guarantee of the individual's liberty. With the rise of capitalism, the marketplace became the arena in which individual freedom was exercised and largely defined. It was seen as the necessary and efficient mechanism to secure and advance the liberty and well-being both of the individual and of society as a whole. This negative view of liberty, virtually synonymous with economic individualism, severely restricted the application of equality.

Liberal thinkers have typically advocated the negative view of liberty, that is, freedom from coercion by other individuals or by the state.[14] They are critical of positive liberty, understood as the maximization of one's powers. Positive liberty is the liberty of the individual to be his or her own master, to act as a fully human being. Liberal thinkers such as Isaiah Berlin contend that positive liberty as a political ideal leads to coercion because it can be used to justify imposing a particular concept of the good on society. The problem with this division of liberty, declares C.B. Macpherson, is that negative liberty has become an ideological justification for "un-individualist, corporate, imperial, 'free enterprise' "[15] and fails to reckon with the way in which socioeconomic conditions interfere with the full development of human powers. Macpherson's point is well taken. Positive liberty entails access to employment and adequate means of life as well as protection against interference with the requirements of self-development. Positive liberty must be sought as a political ideal if persons are to exercise the economic rights necessary for the "pursuit of happiness." [16]

Liberty, Equality, and Slavery

To understand the darker aspect of our national identity, one must ask how a people who professed the political ideals of liberty and equality could tolerate slavery. On the one hand, those ideals enshrined in our founding documents were couched in universal terms; on the other, they were designed to protect the property and secure the liberties of the landed gentry and to exclude women and blacks from political participation in the commonwealth. The issue of constitutional intent came up when President Reagan nominated Judge Robert H. Bork to the U.S. Supreme Court. The dominant question during the hearings was whether the Constitution was to be interpreted according to the "original intent" of the Founders. The most infamous appeal to a jurisprudence of original intent was in the Supreme Court decision that Chief Justice Roger B. Taney wrote for the majority in *Dred Scott* v. *Sandford* (1857). He said:

> The duty of the court is, to interpret the instrument they [the founders] have framed, with the best lights we can obtain on the subject, and to administer it as we find it, according to its true intent and meaning when it was adopted.... It is too clear for dispute, that the enslaved African race were not intended to be included, and formed no part of the people who framed and adopted this declaration [of Independence].... This state of public opinion had undergone no

change when the Constitution was adopted, as is equally evident from its provisions and language.[17]

Although Judge Bork was clearly not in sympathy with this "original intent" of the framers, Justice Taney's prejudicial view reflects a continuing problem in American jurisprudence.

Many of the Founding Fathers were uncomfortable with the institution of slavery. But while Washington, Jefferson, and Madison agonized over their ownership of slaves, they were willing neither to free their own slaves nor to speak out publicly against slavery. "In private," says one historian, Washington "equated manumission with the exercise of 'humanity,' yet he denigrated immediate emancipation as certain to produce 'much inconvenience and mischief,' and he refused to lend his magical name to the cause of gradual emancipation."[18] In retirement Washington kept his bondsmen in order to maintain his accustomed style of life. The ideal of equality was tailored to the exigencies of politics and economics.

The institution of slavery in America was unique, unlike anything seen before or at that time in Africa, Spain, Portugal, and Latin America.[19] Everywhere else, the slave had some social status and legal rights, and there were many points of contact between free persons and those with the legal status of slaves. In the United States, the institution of slavery, under the domination of the planter class, was unrestrained by other institutions. The slaveowner had absolute discretion in the legal categories of the slave's term of servitude, marriage and the family, discipline, and property.[20] Humane considerations were overridden when they conflicted with property rights. For practical purposes and before the law, slaves were unequal because they were not "men."

If by the 1830s Tocqueville found "equality of condition" to be the principle that explained the new American democracy, it was less an inclusive political ideal than a temper of social life in Jacksonian democracy. It had more to do with the new financial independence of a growing number of farmers and tradesmen and the free and easy manners of the people Tocqueville observed than with the enfranchisement of those who had earlier been excluded from the civil community. Tocqueville himself was filled with foreboding as he contemplated the fearful consequences of slavery in America. Political equality would be granted to all citizens with the establishment of civil rights only after years of anguish and struggle. The principle of equality has yet to be applied to economic rights. The question is still not completely resolved in American life as to how many in the society are to count as free and equal citizens of the commonwealth.

Conflict of Values

Fortunately, the Constitution held within it the possibility that the nation might one day choose to act on the Declaration's affirmation "that all men are created equal." The novelist E. L. Doctorow captures its genius when he declares: "That once you write the prophetic text for a true democracy—as our forefathers did in their draft and as our amending legislators and judiciary have continued to do in their editing of its moral self-contradictions and methodological inadequacies—that once this text is in voice, it cannot be said to be realized on earth until all the relations among the American people, legal relations, property relations, are made just."[21] The constitutionally enacted democratic self-identity contained the potentiality of an inclusive community of citizens who would be free and equal. Its realization has been hindered by some fundamental value conflicts in American life, which have to do with the individualism and materialism intrinsic to our economic system and social practices, and which lead us to interpret liberty and equality in restrictive ways.

Even though abundant evidence points to individualism and materialism as central values for Americans, it is obviously wrong to think that they are simple, rigid, or exclusive in their meaning. These values are held along with, and often in tension with, others. Although today some writers see a conflict between old and new values in contemporary society, it is more likely that we are experiencing an intensification of a conflict in values that Americans have held all along.[22]

Fundamental conflicts of value in the culture were seen by the psychoanalyst Karen Horney some forty years ago to be reflected in individual neurosis, which she characterized as "the neurotic personality of our time." Among them was the conflict between competition and success, on the one hand, and brotherly love and humility, on the other. A wealth of research data in psychology and sociology has demonstrated the pernicious effects of this conflict on human personality and development.[23] It is a conflict between the interests one holds as an atomistic individual and as a person in community.

While the underlying conflict in the American value system is not new, it has been increasingly sharpened by the central thrust of industrialization. On the one hand, we have a social order geared to productivity; on the other, a culture oriented to consumption. The socioeconomic order is highly organized, with a premium on rationality; the culture is geared to pleasure, enjoyment, and the enhancement of the self. Daniel Bell describes this as a "disjunction between the social structure and the culture," a crisis in capitalist society brought about by the collapse of the value system that gave rise to capitalism, hard work, thrift, and self-denial. This value system, ironically, has been undermined by capitalism itself. The disjunction will inevitably widen, Bell foresees, with no basis in a postindustrial society for a communal ethic. "The lack of a rooted moral belief system is the cultural contradiction of the society, the deepest challenge to its survival," says Bell.[24] To put it in terms of our historical sketch of the liberal tradition in America: Middle-class morality and rationality have produced a society that threatens those middle-class values believed to be the foundations of a free, just, and humane society—liberty, equality, property, and religion.

In the past several decades, liberalism has come under critical scrutiny because of the limitations and dangers of the atomistic individualism that, in spite of all of its contributions, it has fostered. The realities of a shrinking world, more and more interrelated in commerce and culture, are making many Americans aware of their interdependence. No nation and certainly no group, no matter how economically well off, can insulate itself from the rest of the country or the world. Each is vulnerable to the actions of all others. We are all affected by problems of the decaying infrastructure of the nation's transportation system, water supply, and waste disposal, and by poverty, crime, and racial division. Our inner conflict of values is projected in garish colors on the screen of the city, environment, public life, international relations. Social problems are forcing the question—as it has been forced in crises such as the Revolutionary and Civil wars, the Great Depression, the civil rights struggle—of who we are as a people. At bottom are conflicting root metaphors of who we are as selves.

Root Metaphors of the Self: Atomistic Individualism

Underlying the policy choices we have considered and perhaps all significant public policy decisions is some predominant value assumption about who we are as a people. We may call this a root metaphor of the self. The metaphor that figures prominently in the mainstream American story is that of the self as atomistic individual.

In political individualism, the individual is conceived in abstraction from community and society. Motivated by the desire to acquire possessions for pleasure and for security against the assaults of nature and man, the individual enters into a social contract for protection from the state. Government is based on the consent of citizens, intended to ensure the representation of individual interests, and to enable individuals to satisfy their wants, mainly in the marketplace. The government's role is to protect the life, liberty, and, especially, property of its citizens. Individuals pursue what they want by organizing around common interests in order to compete with others in the play of power. We see ourselves as self-seeking individuals, independent and beholden to no one, responsible alone for our success or failure, free of any bonds but those we voluntarily accept—in short, atomistic individuals. This view shapes public policy, which in turn reinforces that image.

Economic individualism is closely allied with political individualism in the liberal tradition. Since Adam Smith, neoclassical economics has evolved as a system of private property, free exchange, and competition in the marketplace, designed to make the most efficient allocation of resources, to satisfy people's wants. Rationality is tied to self-interest. "Economic man" is rational when he acts to maximize his "utility" (pleasure, preferences, interests).

Psychological individualism has reduced human behavior to individual needs and drives, explaining it in terms of pain and pleasure. Man, according to the dominant psychologies, *is* and *ought* to be selfishly motivated. The moral teachings of culture and religion are viewed as frustrating and oppressive, creating guilt and neurosis. Moral norms inhibit our actions, duty enchains us; we ought to accept our biological and psychological impulses as good and seek pleasure.[25]

This psychological view of the human being as a selfish, pleasure-seeking individual is not alien to traditional religion (compare, for example, the Christian doctrine of original sin). The crucial difference is in the normative doctrine of individualistic psychology as opposed to that of religion. Psychiatry and psychology are oriented to the individual's self-expression; religion is oriented to that which enhances community. My purpose here is not to offer a moral critique of the "pleasure principle" in psychology or the pursuit of pleasure by the individual but to underscore the way in which individualism in psychological theory undermines the notion of moral community.

The negative view of morality in contemporary psychology has been transmitted to college undergraduates and to more and more secondary school pupils.[26] When students are socialized into a negative view of the socialization process, psychologists themselves may begin to express concern over the results. As Arthur Koestler once said in a BBC broadcast, if you teach students that they are rats, do not be surprised if they grow whiskers and bite your hand! Donald Campbell strongly recommends to his fellow psychologists that they exercise caution in opposing traditional moralizing and respect the "underlying wisdom in the recipes for living with which tradition has supplied us."[27]

The Metaphor as Model

We Americans are socialized into an image of ourselves as atomistic individuals by the way we conceive of our core values of liberty, equality, property, and religion; by our national ideology, which identifies the individual with the nation, which is number one; by popular culture (Hollywood, advertising, television, radio, recordings) in images such as the Lone Ranger, Rambo, Superman, John Wayne, Ronald Reagan, Lee Iacocca, Ivan Boesky, and J.R. Ewing; and by social scientific models of the self. When we add the social science disciplines together, especially those of psychology and economics, we find them converging on a model of human nature as self-interested and acquisitive, an atomistic individual abstracted from history and from all that makes a person identifiable, known, and respected and cared for as a person. The economic individual motivated solely by rational calculation of narrow self-interest is an "unencumbered self," without friendships, loves, loyalties, values, obligations, and commitments.[28] The result is a concept of the self that influences our actions and our public policy.

This view of the self as independent, self-interested, economically motivated, and exclusive of others is a view we all understand and in some measure live. It is enshrined in popular thought and social scientific theory as "human nature." Its version in economic theory has shaped public policy and dominated the moral imagination. It does not, however, account for the full range of human experience. Such a two-dimensional view affords no explanation for why a person salutes the flag, stops to help a stranded motorist, volunteers several hours a week in a soup kitchen, votes for aid to the indigent, or simply votes at all. This model of the self does not tally with the way we live our lives when we find them most satisfying and fulfilling.

Decency, fair play, and concern for the weak, the helpless, and the oppressed are native to the American moral tradition and grounded in the Judeo-Christian tradition of justice and mercy. Even economic theorists themselves have traditionally invoked the sanction of moral values, either tacitly or explicitly, for example, as implied in the term *welfare economics*. The economic mode of rationality with its associated values of hard work, competition, and achievement is regnant but not absolute in American society.

The motive of private self-interest operating in the market economy is not sufficient to secure the public goods that individuals may desire. Theorists of the "free rider" problem observe that the individual will not be moved to sacrifice strong and immediate self-interest for a desirable but remote collective good, even when it is in that individual's interest. When the individual can enjoy some benefits independent of his or her own contribution, it would not seem to be "rational" to make a voluntary contribution to collective welfare.[29] In fact, however, people act not simply as self-interested individuals but as members of a community, sharing some common values, commitments, and obligations. People vote regularly, knowing that their individual votes will not affect the outcome of the election. In time of crisis they rally to help the victims of catastrophe. They respond to charity drives and give to philanthropic causes. They have a sense of decency and fairness that will lead them to support a social system that is responsive to people's needs.

The Self as Person-in-Community

We have to acknowledge certain aspects of ourselves in the model of the self as atomistic individual. But it is also necessary to recognize large tracts of our experience that are not explained or illuminated by that image. Self-interest is far broader, more comprehensive than that of economic individualism, and it is realized in the universe of relations with others. We are not simply, and not mainly, rational interest maximizers. We are moved by duty as well as pleasure, by what we think is right as well as by what we prefer. We do not act as lone individuals but as persons whose interests and values are shaped by the communities of which we are members and by society. As we look outward, we find ourselves expanded as selves, with more capacity for suffering and for joy, for giving and for receiving.

The psychologist Gordon Allport observed that the universal hunger for love in human nature has not been sufficiently recognized by psychologists. Modern psychology reacted to theology and Christianity's emphasis on love with a "flight from tenderness," as one writer suggested. But Allport insisted that desires for affiliation are so fundamental that they are taken for granted. Studies indicate that persons seek friendly relations with others as long as their own sense of self-esteem and integrity is preserved.[30] Much social science research supports the view that human well-being depends both on affiliative relations with others and on self-love and self-esteem. It confirms traditional religious wisdom in stressing the importance of the nurturing community for moral development. As Erik Erikson has said: "There is much in ancient wisdom which now, perhaps, can become knowledge."[31]

"A person is a personality," George H. Mead has said, "because he belongs to a community, because he takes over the institutions of that community into his own conduct."[32] Without the human virtues of care and competence, institutions wilt, says Erikson, "but without the spirit of institutions pervading the patterns of care, love, instruction and training, no virtue could emerge from the sequence of generations."[33] The principle of mutuality is the essence of the Golden Rule, a religious formulation of the insight that mutuality strengthens both the doer and the other.

An image of the self that accords with who we are and is large enough to suggest possibilities for action on behalf of others in public life must be an inclusive one. It will include the self-interested and the relational self, a comprehensive and contextual understanding of the self as person-in-community, moral actor, and citizen of the commonwealth. This requires some imagination. When our imaginations are dominated by the metaphor of the marketplace, we are likely to act as anxious and hostile competitors in an economy of scarcity. It takes an act of will inspired by a healthy and creative imagination to conceive of ourselves as citizens in an inclusive community, members of a commonwealth.

Interests and Values

We are not simply propelled by interests as atomistic individuals; we are also impelled by values, as members of communities. In general usage, *value* refers to a standard of worth. But because it is a key word in the vocabulary of economics and in popular parlance frequently connotes an economic standard of worth, value tends to be equated with *interest*. The philosophical and moral meanings of value are, however, much broader and should be distinguished from the idea of economic interest. Interests are arbitrary preferences, defined as the individual desires. Values, by contrast, are believed to be desirable in themselves, apart from whether they are in fact preferred by all. We desire the freedom and the right to pursue our interests, but we believe that there are values that ought to be recognized and accepted, preserved and enhanced by everyone. This distinction is vitally important in the realm of public life and collective decision making. As citizens, we may not agree with the interests of others, but we affirm their right to pursue those interests. Politics and the marketplace provide arenas in which those with competing interests engage in the "play of power." These political and economic "mechanisms" will continue to work, however, only as long as they are sustained on the basis of shared values of liberty and equality, justice and the common good. These values, and certain others also, are good and desirable, essential to the public realm.

Value discourse, in contrast with the pursuit of interest, requires a community with a shared tradition. A communal perspective is needed for an appreciation of values that from an individualistic point of view are reduced to matters of taste, preference, and interest. The marketplace is an efficient arrangement for the satisfaction of economic interests. The realization of values, however, is contingent on an ongoing public conversation about the symbols, ideals, principles, and ideas of the culture. Values as well as interests influence the formation of institutions, the use of resources, the distribution of wealth, and the treatment of people. But they are achieved not through power alone but by persuasion. They elicit cooperation in the effort to attain them.

Collectivity of Individuals or Commonwealth?

Configurations of value shape our identity as citizens, our understanding of social problems, and the limits of our community. The social problem of poverty, for example, is often defined in individualistic terms, as though the individual were wholly responsible for his or her plight. Individuals and groups are judged by consensual (majoritarian or elitist) values and found wanting. Society blames the victims.[34] They are poor because they are lazy and apathetic. They prefer instant rather than delayed gratification. They spend money on the wrong things. They are sick because they do not take care of themselves. Their children drop out of school because they are genetically or culturally inferior and lack ambition and motivation. Whatever basis this litany of stereotypes may have in fact, it derives not from the values of the "subculture" of the poor but from the intractable problems of being poor. As has been said, the trouble with being poor is that you don't have money. There is sociological evidence that the poor in fact share the values of mainstream America.[35] The behavior of most poor people results, not from their rejection of the majoritarian values of the work ethic, but from their inability to find and keep a decent job. The fundamental social problem is not the habits and values of the poor but their lack of economic and social opportunity.

The way we understand our values, individualistically or communally, determines our identity as citizens and sets the limits of our community. As atomistic individual, one is a consumer of goods and services; as citizen, one is accountable to all other citizens in the public realm. Accountability means that all must *count,* they must be included as free and equal citizens in the civil community. Each has a stake in civil community—and the community has a stake in each citizen. Insofar as an individual is alienated or excluded from the community, that one is a threat to the community. The problems of crime and, increasingly, of terrorism, evidence the community's dire need to give everyone a genuine stake in the community.

The political issue is finally one of social membership. When people are excluded from active participation in the economic and political community, they suffer a sense of isolation and alienation that can lead to resentment and violence. Sabotage has plagued some of the largest and most efficient automobile manufacturing plants, evidence of the dehumanization of the workplace. Compared to that of many European countries, American productivity does not suffer as much from inferior technology as it does from poorer motivation, less cooperation, and adversarial rather than teamwork relations, according to the economist Lester Thurow.[36] The revitalization of industry and of politics will come only when workers and citizens share a collective sense of purpose, supported by mutual trust and shared responsibility in the making of decisions affecting the commonwealth.[37]

The fundamental issue underlying virtually every public policy decision is Who counts? Inclusion as a vote is not enough. Voices must count: respect for the expressed interests and recognition of the needs of all; the opportunity for those voices to be heard and included in policy debate; an accounting for decisions reached—a justification of the reasoning and the values. If voices are truly to count, the *meaning* of what they say must be taken into account in the public forum. This presupposes more than a commercial society of self-seeking individuals, a civil community of persons who reason together about values.

The good of all is the proper end of a self-governed people who, at least in the early days of the Republic, thought of themselves as a "commonwealth." The term was widely used in the New England states in the early nineteenth century in reference to community measures of health and safety. Under the commonwealth doctrine, group interests took precedence over private interests when the legislature so chose, for there was general recognition that there were goods that individuals could only achieve together, as a community. In our own time, when private greed has been praised as the stimulus to national wealth, the consequences of unrestrained possessive individualism may make the notion of common-wealth more attractive and even compelling. In a commonwealth, citizens seek their common interests as well as their individual and private inter-ests.

Who Are We?

Here we might perform a thought experiment. We may ask, What mini-mal value-identity is required of a citizen and of a society in order to achieve and maintain a quality of life desired by the members of that soci-ety? Specifically, how much of the following passage would it be necessary for a people to affirm in order to ensure a just and peaceful society?

> The dignity of the human person, realized in community with others, is the criterion against which all aspects of economic life must be measured. All human beings, therefore, are ends to be served by the institutions that make up the economy, not means to be exploited for more narrowly defined goals. Human personhood must be respected with a reverence that is religious. When we deal with each other, we should do so with the sense of awe that arises in the presence of something holy and sacred. For that is what human beings are: we are created in the image of God (Gen. 1:27). Similarly, all economic in-stitutions must support the bonds of community and solidarity that are essential to the dignity of persons. Wherever our economic arrange-ments fail to conform to the demands of human dignity lived in com-munity, they must be questioned and transformed. These convictions have a biblical basis. They are also supported by a long tradition of theological and philosophical reflection and through the reasoned analysis of human experience by contemporary men and women.[38]

This passage may provoke reflection on and a critical analysis of the values we would ourselves affirm as the basis for a good and just society. The exercise is not simply theoretical, for our choices reflect our values. And by our personal and policy decisions we choose who we are as a people. It may be worthwhile, therefore, to examine the Pastoral Letter on Economic Justice by Roman Catholic Bishops in America, *Economic Justice for All,* in which this passage occurs.

Religion and Property: A Vision of Economic Justice

A comprehensive vision of the public good is not encouraged by the pragmatic and incremental approach to politics in America. From time to time, however, there are those who envision what the society as a whole could be. It was a historic event when, in November 1980, the Roman Catholic bishops of the United States decided to write a letter on the U.S. economy. Four years later, after extensive study and consultation, they released the first draft of the Pastoral Letter on Catholic Social Teaching and the U.S. Economy. The bishops called for increased financial support of programs to help the sick, poor, and jobless just as the Reagan administration was preparing to cut spending on school aid, nutrition plans, health care, and other programs. The pastoral letter immediately became an influential part of the national economic debate.[39] The bishops invited interested readers of the letter, Catholics and others, to respond with suggestions for improving it. Debates ensued in schools, unions, classrooms, boardrooms, national journals, and on television. The bishops' national offices received 10,000 pages of responses. After studying these and discussing the important issues in June 1985, the committee wrote a second draft of the letter, which appeared on 7 October 1985.[40] Again responses were invited for help in preparing the final draft, which the bishops were to make public in the summer of 1986 and on which, after further discussion, they would vote final acceptance in their meeting on November 1986.

The document was noteworthy for its aim, its content, and its reception. It offered a moral vision of the nation in which a more just economy would be at the service of all people, especially the poor. The bishops declared: "This document is not a technical blueprint for economic reform, and it does not provide definitive solutions to the problems discussed. Rather, it is an attempt to foster a serious moral analysis of economic justice."[41]

To that end, the bishops proposed basic moral norms, but they also made prudential judgments, recognizing that the credibility of the document would depend on their making specific applications of their principles. Their first draft was criticized by many as naive and simplistic. These criticisms were muted when a number of well-known economists, including Nobel laureates James Tobin and Lawrence R. Klein, rallied to its support.[42]

The pastoral letter represents a historic contribution by a religious community to the policy-making process. Its "Christian vision of economic life" is based on the long tradition of Christian teaching and reflection on economic life, as well as on the common moral ground Americans share. Its principle of coherence and fundamental criterion of economic life is "the dignity of the human person, realized in community with others."[43] The bishops appeal to Christians and to all in the pluralist society to show the respect and reverence owed to the dignity of every person.

The ethical framework for guiding economic life consists of the duties of love and justice that people owe one another and the protection of the human rights of all persons. Translated into moral priorities for the nation, this implies special duties toward the economically vulnerable. There are 33 million Americans who are poor (living at or below the poverty line) and another 20 to 30 million who are needy. Between 1979 and 1983, there was an increase of over 9 million people living in poverty by the government's definition. "That so many people are poor in a nation as rich as ours," say the bishops, "is a social and moral scandal that must not be ignored."[44]

The poor have the most urgent claim on the national conscience, since material deprivation compounds all other kinds of suffering. Justice mandates a fundamental "option for the poor," the obligation to view economic activity from the standpoint of the powerless. The bishops do not wish to pit groups against one another; instead, they insist that the disabilities of any affect the good of the whole.

Fulfilling the basic needs of the poor takes highest priority on the policy agenda. A second priority is that of enhancing economic participation through ensuring employment for those denied jobs by no fault of their own. A third priority is investment in education, health, and other resources needed to benefit the poor. The experiment in civil and political rights needs to be matched by a similar experiment in securing economic rights: "the creation of an order that guarantees the minimum conditions of human dignity in the economic sphere for every person."[45]

In the light of their moral vision, ethical norms, and priorities for economic life, the bishops select four economic policy issues: employment, poverty, food and agriculture, and international economic concerns. Full employment is the most urgent domestic economic priority, calling for national fiscal and monetary policies in order to achieve it. Job-training and direct job-creation programs are needed, along with new strategies in such areas as job sharing, a reduced workweek, reducing wage differentials between the sexes, and improving occupational safety. A national strategy against poverty would foster self-help efforts among the poor, reduce their tax burden, support and strengthen their families, and provide adequate levels of support to cover basic needs. Agricultural policy should be designed to protect moderate-size and small farms by tax reform, research, improvement of productivity, and protection of farm workers, especially migratory field workers. The United States also has a responsibility in the international economic system, which should be determined by human need, not "national security." The policy imperative of a "preferential option for the poor" invoked in regard to domestic policy applies to aid to developing nations as well.

The bishops conclude their letter by sketching the outlines of a "partnership for the public good." This entails the development of new institutional structures in order to distribute economic power more widely and justly. All parts of society must cooperate in forming national economic policies. The Catholic "principle of subsidiarity" is relevant in determining the role of the state in these needed reforms. The government should do for individuals and groups only what they cannot do for themselves in securing justice and human rights. It should encourage cooperation and help groups contribute to the common good.

The pastoral letter combines moral vision with a realistic appraisal of the way in which the economic system affects the well-being of American citizens. While evoking criticism and debate, it sets forth an impressive vision of the public good that is animated by the spirit of a religious community with a long and rich tradition of ethical reflection. It is not, however, bound by the religious beliefs of that community but embraces moral concerns and articulates a moral vision that can be shared by all Americans. At a time when national preoccupation with individual wealth seeking seems to have eclipsed the ideals of the commonwealth, the Roman Catholic bishops effectively raised the ethical question of economic justice to the level of public discussion.

The bishops' letter has been criticized as too idealistic. Its application of religious and public ethics to the just use of property does represent a vision still to be realized of what America should be. But the history of a city forced to integrate its schools by busing students demonstrates that the political values of liberty and equality can be applied in the struggle to achieve an inclusive community.

Liberty and Equality: A City Chooses What It Will Be

In Charlotte, North Carolina, in 1971, a U.S. Supreme Court decision, *Swann* v. *Charlotte-Mecklenburg,* mandated integration of the schools, with the use of busing if necessary. The story of the decade that followed is one of tension and conflict, of fear and uncertainty, of conflicting views of what the city should be. But it is also a story of people who found that what they had in common was more important than what separated them. It is the story of a city's agonizing but successful attempt to decide who it would be as a people.[46]

The case that reached the Supreme Court began with the lawsuit of Darius and Vera Swann. The Swanns had lived as the only blacks in a missionary community in India. On furlough in Charlotte, they found that their son was not allowed to attend the school closest to their home. When school officials refused their request for him to attend the school, the Swanns brought suit in 1965. There were limited results, and the case was reopened in 1968 before Federal Judge James B. McMillan, who rendered his decision on 23 April 1969.

Judge McMillan asserted that in spite of some progress since the 1965 ruling, the Charlotte-Mecklenburg school system was not yet desegregated. In his twenty-one-page court order, Judge McMillan cited discrimination in private facilities and public zoning and planning, and the effects of urban renewal and public housing in concentrating blacks in certain areas of the city as causes of segregated housing. He acknowledged the efforts that the city had made to accommodate itself to the law regarding desegregation but declared that there was a duty to do more than "refrain from active legal racial discrimination." There was now "a duty to act positively to fashion affirmatively a school system as free as possible from the lasting effects of such historical *apartheid*." He observed that "the Board has the power to use buses for all legitimate school purposes. Buses for many years were used to operate segregated schools. There is no reason except emotion (and I confess to having felt my own share of emotion on this subject in all the years before I studied the facts) why school buses can not be used by the Board to provide the flexibility and economy necessary to desegregate the schools."[47]

The case was appealed to the U.S. Supreme Court, and on 20 April 1971 the Court affirmed the order of the district court. For the next five years, Judge McMillan steadfastly adhered to the intent of his ruling, in spite of vehement opposition. But while the matter was settled in the courts, it had yet to be worked out in the city. Bitter resistance to the Court's decree included a series of maneuvers by the Board intended to forestall busing. Judge McMillan was harassed and threatened on numerous occasions. There were several violent incidents in the schools. The homes of a number of black leaders were bombed, and the office of Julius Chambers, attorney for the plaintiff, was burned. In the midst of this unhappy period of racial tension and animosity, however, there were blacks and whites, some civic leaders and others ordinary citizens, who recognized the justice of the Court's decision. Even some of those who thought busing was the wrong way to achieve desegregation, like W. T. Harris, chairman of the Mecklenburg Board of County Commissioners, came to accept it. "We've got to stand where the law is," Harris said, "not just where we would like it to be."[48]

As judge and school board struggled to work out a mutually agreeable plan through the summer of 1973, citizens in various parts of Charlotte were beginning to speak up for "fairness and stability," a new slogan that captured the spirit of those who were facing up to the responsibilities of change. By 1975 the school board submitted a proposal worked out with the Citizens Advisory Group, Judge McMillan approved it and after observing the way it worked over the next year, announced on 11 July 1976 that he was closing his file on the case.

The reporter who covered the course of *Swann* called the years following the Court's decision "the golden decade." Test scores rose, along
with the satisfaction and pride of students and parents. Coalitions of blacks
and whites formed throughout the city and began to work for goals beyond the schools. A grass-roots movement succeeded in changing the
election of the City Council (mainly white businessmen) by a referendum.
A system of district representation replaced election of representatives at
large, thereby ensuring a wider and more diverse representation on the
City Council. A black councilman, Harvey Gantt, was elected mayor in
1983 and in 1985, even though over 75 percent of Charlotte's voters were
white. There were still problems, but the city was by general agreement a
stronger and better city than it had been before the *Swann* decision. How
did it happen?

For a variety of reasons, some of them having to do with a subsequent conservative retrenchment by the Supreme Court, busing did not
work as well in some other major cities across the country. Boston was the
most notorious example, where the court plan largely exempted affluent
areas of the city and allowed the burden to fall on blacks and whites in the
lower-income districts of South Boston and Roxbury. In Charlotte, Judge
McMillan insisted that every district of the city be included in busing, to
prevent "white flight." A large part of Charlotte's success reflected the
willingness of Judge McMillan to work closely with those who felt initially
that the proposed solution was unfair. Charlotte had something else—a
history of good-faith efforts on the part of city leaders to desegregate
schools and public facilities. A token beginning was made in 1957 when
Dorothy Counts enrolled at Harding High School. Because of harassment,
her parents transferred her. City and county schools were consolidated in a
special referendum in 1959.

Several school administrators who committed themselves to the process of desegregation in the years following had the support of other city
leaders, including the mayor. Pete McKnight, editor of the *Charlotte Observer,* led the way with editorials that took a forthright stand for desegregation, dating from before the desegregation decision of the Supreme Court
in 1954. He was instrumental in getting the Chamber of Commerce to
call for voluntary desegregation of public accommodations, which Chamber leaders took immediate steps to implement. During the stressful years

in which almost all the white citizens were critical of Judge McMillan's decision, McKnight actively continued to give editorial support for desegregation by busing. Gene Owen, minister of the prestigious Myers Park Baptist Church, was another who, with several other ministers, gave Judge McMillan public support.

A critical factor in the achievement of integration was the emergence of leaders in the citizen coalitions concerned with education. One of the most effective was Maggie Ray, a young housewife, who became the leader of the Citizens Advisory Group. This was a semiofficial group that was to help the school board come up with a new plan for integration. The plan that was finally accepted was the product of the intensive work of this group with a committee chaired by Assistant Superintendent of Schools John Phillips.

After all the prominent figures in the drama of desegregation have been noted, it is the lawyer for the plaintiff and the federal judge who remain the central figures. Julius Chambers, the brilliant young black lawyer who prepared the case and eventually argued it before the Supreme Court, was well prepared by ability, temperament, self-discipline, and courage to see the case through. His tenacity was matched with the toughness—some called it stubbornness—of Judge James McMillan. Judge McMillan had not been an advocate of busing. But once persuaded by the facts and his finely honed sense of legal justice, he held firmly to his goal. Just as important, however, he sought to elicit the cooperation of the community in working out reasonable and effective means of achieving the goal.

Judge McMillan's decree forced Charlotte to choose what kind of city—what kind of people—it would be. It was a southern city, with racism entrenched in attitudes and institutions. It was also a city with much goodwill, with a tradition of tolerance and strong civic pride. In the crises precipitated by the courts, city leaders would appeal to enlightened self-interest, the need to support the schools both for the economic health of the community and out of civic duty. There was something else. Though it is understated and mainly alluded to without comment, the thread of religious faith and conviction runs through the whole story, in the account of the author, Frye Gaillard, from his introduction of the federal judge as "a soft-spoken Presbyterian named James B. McMillan" to W. T. Harris's remonstrance to his friend Bill Poe, who was continuing to resist the judge's order: "Bill, how in the world do you justify this? I'm a Christian. I couldn't sleep at night."[49] When Charlotte found itself in the moment of crisis (a word that in Chinese means "danger and opportunity"), there were resources of law, morality, and religion on which people drew in acting on their choices.

The Charlotte story was, as an editorial writer on the *Observer* called it, a classic case study in the workings of democracy. It began with black citizens who pressed their claims for equality of treatment for all and who persisted in spite of phenomenal obstacles. Groups contended for their interests, some of them narrowly conceived. Big ideas and fundamental American values were at stake, some in seeming conflict with each other. Lawyers, judge, and school board were central, but civic leaders and countless citizens played their parts. Policy was made, not by scientific rationality or by the application of abstract ethical principles elegantly formulated, but by a legal process that involved the whole community. Its outcome reflected a sense of fairness, civic pride, enlightened self-interest, and hope for the future. It was the choice of Charlotte to be an inclusive community, committed to the welfare of all.

When President Reagan stopped in Charlotte to address a campaign rally in the fall of 1984, in a remark aimed at the Democrats, he criticized those supporting busing. Busing, he said, "takes innocent children out of the neighborhood school and makes them pawns in a social experiment that nobody wants. And we've found out that it failed." The *Charlotte Observer* replied the next day with an editorial headed "You Were Wrong, Mr. President":

> Charlotte-Mecklenburg's proudest achievement of the past 20 years is not the city's impressive new skyline or its strong, growing economy. Its proudest achievement is its fully integrated school system. That system was born out of bitter controversy over court-ordered busing. It was shaped by caring citizens who refused to see their schools and their community torn apart by racial conflict. It was nourished by courageous elected officials, creative school administrators and dedicated teachers and parents. It has blossomed into one of the nation's finest, recognized through the United States for quality, innovation

and, most of all, for overcoming the most difficult challenge American public education has ever faced.[50]

The future of the Charlotte schools is not assured, for "the very fact of two races living side by side would require an ongoing vigilance against the worst that's still within us," says author Gaillard.[51] But when Vice-President Dan Quayle spoke in Charlotte in the spring of 1989, incredibly he repeated the assertion that mandatory busing to achieve school desegregation had not been a success. Replaying the former President's remarks, Quayle said: "Even those who initially promoted that as a way to achieve desegregation have admitted that it has not been a successful tool to achieve that objective." But, as the *Observer* reported, Ashley L. Hogewood, Jr., chairman of the Charlotte-Mecklenburg school board, said he thought Mr. Quayle "fell into the trap of using the hackneyed phrase that it's a social experiment. Well, it's not an experiment in Charlotte-Mecklenburg. It's a way of life."[52]

It is a way of life that demonstrates how a city can together work through the obstacles to community justice, peace, and stability, with the dividend of a higher quality of education and life.

Conclusion

By our policy decisions, we decide who we are as a people. Our identity may be shaped by our values, by metaphor, myth, and story, but it becomes palpable and institutionalized by conscious decision, that is, by policy making. In policy choices we are responsible for deciding who we will be. In this chapter we have considered how our American sense of identity, national and personal, has been conceived largely in terms of economic individualism. Our atomistic individualism is not something that we have reflected on and decided to adopt as a metaphor by which to live. It is, in fact, more than a metaphor, it is a myth that pervades our whole way of life, that determines our view of the world and that is the preconscious assumption on which we base our corporate policy decisions. As a myth, it is a way of experiencing the world. We cannot escape that myth simply by intellectual analysis, any more than one can extricate oneself from an Oedipal complex by reading Freud. So pervasive and unchallengeable is the myth of individualism that it constitutes a kind of American religion, a civil religion that binds us together in our ineluctable separatenesses as a "lonely crowd."

How can we possibly extricate ourselves from a myth as far reaching in its domination of our moral imagination and as powerful in its stultifying effect on the public realm as the myth of atomistic individualism? No intellectual examination, no matter how probing, could disclose the myriad ways in which that myth has constrained us, Gullivers bound by Lilliputian threads too numerous and too subtle for us to be able ever to sever them one by one. Critical analysis of our American moral tradition, of our political and economic ideology, our popular culture, our social scientific models of the self, the education through which we have become socialized into our self-identity as atomistic individuals, will not be enough to deliver us from the narrow confines and the isolation of the alienated self.

The myth of individualism may retain its grip until we are forced by mounting difficulties to recognize its fatal limitations. It reinforces in us those resistances to community enterprises that keep us from acknowledging the immense problems that face our cities, nation, and planet. They are problems that we read about every day, that are graphically pictured in the evening news, that lie uneasily in the back of our minds, but that we refuse to face with a view to action. To deal with them will require a willingness to pay for the measures necessary to deal with the breakdown of the infrastructure of our cities, the poisoning of our underground water tables, the degradation of our urban landscape, the festering of our ghettoes. Even more, it will require a fundamental change in our style of life: a concern with conservation, rather than unlimited consumption; cooperation in working out collective solutions, rather than competition in seeing how much we can get for ourselves in "working the system"; self-discipline, rather than self-indulgence.

Only a view of the self more compelling, more adequate to the realities of our lives, more authentic, can successfully challenge the myth of individualism. To choose ourselves as relational beings, persons-in-community, is not to fabricate an ideal model. It is to recognize what we genuinely are in our essential way of being in the world. The reality of inescapable community in practical life needs to be tapped to oppose the myth of individualism, so deeply entrenched in American history. In order to do that we will have to give our attention to alternative myths and stories, such as the story of Charlotte-Mecklenburg, which with its community-minded citizens denies the myth of the atomistic individual.

The individualistic, negative view of liberty and equality is bankrupt. It has made us prisoners of the self, rationalizing our bondage to self-centeredness with the name of freedom. But we may conceive our liberty and equality in a much more spacious way, as communal and positive, the necessary and true conditions for the development of the person. Freedom is life turned outward toward others. We cannot *think* our way out of the prison of the self. Freedom comes with a dream; it breathes the air of possibility; it begins with what we *see*. And when we look for those persons and those moments that have graced our lives with a sense of the possible, that have given us the strength and inspiration to act on behalf of others, no matter how we fumble in doing it, that have put us in touch with our larger selves, then we begin to get our bearings and an authentic sense of what we ought to be about. We are prepared to choose ourselves as members of an inclusive community and to apply our American values of liberty, equality, and property in the light of that membership. Martin Luther King, Jr., spoke for all Americans in his speech in Washington, D.C., on 28 August 1963: "I have a dream that one day this nation will rise up and live out the true meaning of its creed: 'We hold these truths to be self-evident, that all men are created equal.'"

5

STARTING FROM HERE

ONE MUST HAVE self-knowledge in order to act ethically. To know who you are, to have an understanding of your situation, and to assume responsibility for what you know is to be prepared to act as citizen in the public realm. These preconditions to ethical action are today ambiguous and confused. The culture of modernity has made it increasingly difficult to stay in touch with our moral selves and to maintain our personal stake in what we know. Our knowledge appears objective and alien to our personal lives and distracts us from the quest for what is good for us and for our fellow citizens. We have largely lost the ethical view of the public.

Unless the "public" is understood ethically, there is no moral basis for citizenship. Søren Kierkegaard in early-nineteenth-century Denmark observed that the modern world differs from the ancient in that "the whole" is no longer concrete. The public is neither a community nor a society, neither a generation nor particular men. It is, he said, an abstraction, a "phantom." Whereas in antiquity the whole consisted of people related to one another as real persons, who acted with a sense of responsibility to each other and who had to submit to the moral judgment of others, the public today is a creation of the press, "consisting of unreal individuals who never are and never can be united in an actual situation or organization—and yet are held together as a whole."[1] The idea of community or of association could not save the age, in Kierkegaard's view: "It is only after the individual has acquired an ethical outlook, in face of the whole world, that there can be any suggestion of really joining together."[2]

While the public realm may lack moral cohesion, it is not possible to draw a sharp division between public and private spheres. I cannot detach myself from the "public" because it informs my consciousness, the intellectual and emotional tone of my inner life, as well as my workaday life. But for my own integrity and individuality I must identify myself in relation to it. I must choose myself. Only then will I be able to make ethical choices about issues of public moment. Only then can I answer the question What am I to do?

This is a dialectical process. I cannot choose myself independently of the public, in the sense of the political culture. And I cannot critically assess the culture without some independence from it. When I understand myself in this way, I become aware of the need to evaluate more consciously and critically the images that infiltrate my consciousness subliminally and shape my self-understanding. Without a recovery of the ethical self, citizens will not hold one another accountable for what they know.

The Information Society

Mutual accountability is necessary for a democratic society, but it is not something that can be taken for granted. The advent of the "information society" makes that accountability all the more tenuous. During the 1970s, American society was frequently characterized as the "knowledge society." Then came the "information explosion." We now live in the "information society." Students, as well as the rest of us, are bombarded with information. We suffer from "information overload." We depend on vast computerized networks of information and are vulnerable to the perturbations in those networks, as was seen on Black Monday, 19 October 1987, when worldwide computer networks triggered the precipitous drop in prices on the stock market. It is yet too soon for us to comprehend all that our new reliance upon computerized information portends, but there are intimations of its significance.

The twentieth century has seen a change in the concept of knowledge that has its roots in the Enlightenment but that reached its extreme limits in the positivist theory propounded in the 1930s. This view reduced knowledge to statements of fact that could be empirically proved, holding that all other statements were either tautological or emotive. This division of fact from value led to a "value-free" view of knowledge, making knowledge (of facts) public and banishing value to the underground of private subjectivity. Long after this early simple-minded positivism was dis-credited—after all, on such grounds, the very theory of positivism itself would be invalidated as knowledge—it had entered popular culture as a truism. With the advent of the mass media and computerization and the reduction of knowledge to information, what had been a theory with a brief academic history became a general cultural experience. Knowledge as rooted in history, transmitted in communal settings with contexts giving it meaning and value, *personal* knowledge, was transmogrified into informa-tion. It follows, though at first it may seem odd, that information is knowledge without value (insofar as it is knowledge without context). The positivist view of knowledge now enculturated as information is a view of knowledge as independent of the knower—objective, impersonal, and value free.

There are problems with this view of knowledge as information, in addition to the fact that it is not true. One problem is that now, in the university and in society, knowledge as information is free floating, while *interests* are attached. Knowledge is seen as public property, but who as-sumes responsibility for it, and how do we hold persons accountable for knowledge? In the information society it is increasingly difficult to hold anyone accountable for knowledge. A most fateful decision is made when fact is divided from value. Value is then frosting on the cake—or it is like the smile on the face of the Cheshire cat, which remains after the cat has disappeared. Again, it is like the question that the ethicist raises after the decision has already been made by scientist, engineer, businessman, and politician.

Values are thought to be private, up to the individual, a mere per-sonal preference, a matter of taste, a statement of opinion only. Of course the "public interest" is free floating because it is a *value*, not backed by the political power of any special interest group. But "private interests" insert themselves into the public sphere and influence the lives of all in countless ways. Interests are advanced by power, while ideas and values depend on thought and can be promoted only in a community of people who think for themselves and with others. This kind of knowledge is personal, social, historical, contextual, and moral. It is the kind of knowledge implied in the ethical question *What is my personal relation to what I know?*

The ethical question leads me to acknowledge what I know to be true, that I am continuously making evaluations and that my facts are the product of my evaluations. This knowledge is fundamentally personal. It will not allow me to let others reduce my responsibility for what I know by dividing fact and value, the first to be determined by someone else (scientist, textbook writer, journalist or television anchorman) and the second up to me (as private individual). This personal knowledge embraces what used to be called *wisdom,* moral knowledge that grasps the larger meaning of our endeavors, including our goals and their implications for our common life. It requires me to try to distinguish between the genuine and the meretricious, between mere appearance and reality. Plato may have had more confidence than we in the human ability to discern the difference between these, but our well-being and perhaps even our survival depend on it. This critical faculty of discerning the truth is tested more than ever in our culture as the line between politics and fiction becomes blurred. Consider the relation between media image and reality.

The Television Culture

The media purport to convey reality by word and image. When the two present conflicting messages, however, it is clear which one is dominant. The dramatic and colorful image eclipses the verbal text. This is well illustrated in an experience recounted by Leslie Stahl, a CBS correspondent who covered the 1984 presidential campaign. In a piece for television in which she described how his staff packaged Mr. Reagan's speeches in beguiling visual images, Ms. Stahl called attention to the ways in which his aides emphasized the president's "greatest asset," his personality. "They also aim to erase the negative," said Stahl, in her commentary. "Mr. Reagan tried to counter the memory of an unpopular issue with a carefully chosen backdrop that actually contradicts the President's policy. Look at the handicapped Olympics, or the opening ceremony of an old-age home. No hint that he tried to cut the budgets for the disabled and for federally subsidized housing for the elderly."[3] In the background of the scene Stahl was describing were red, white, and blue balloons, along with jets overhead, crowds with waving flags, and an Olympic torch, all graphic evidence supporting her charge. Stahl expected a strong negative reaction from Reagan's staff, but to her surprise they were delighted with the piece. They knew that the patriotic images would override what the commentator said.[4] The misleading image was more persuasive than the facts.

The lack of fit between symbol and reality was demonstrated in the next presidential campaign, in the fall of 1988, when early in the campaign Vice-President George Bush called for the daily recitation of the Pledge of Allegiance in schools. He made the Pledge a test of patriotism, which by implication raised a question about his opponent for not making it an issue in his campaign. Apparently no one in either party pointed out that the Pledge was not written until 1892, or that the author was Francis Bellamy, president of the Christian Socialist League and author of *Jesus the Socialist.* More to the point, neither Republicans nor Democrats had anything to say about the *substance* of the Pledge of Allegiance. It served simply as an ideological *sign,* not as a genuine symbol, in which one participates in its meaning.[5] Consider, however, what the Pledge of Allegiance could mean in a political campaign in which issues of justice and liberty were debated in terms of concrete policies. The Pledge serves as a symbol of the moral task confronting America: to turn a vacuous sign into a true symbol of America by implementing the ideals and principles of "liberty and justice for all." Were the Pledge of Allegiance to be used in this way, citizens would have a realistic notion of the kind of candidate they were voting for. Image would reflect reality.

"Most of what candidates do is aimed at your television screen," began a Bruce Morton report on the "CBS Evening News" during the presidential campaign of 1988.[6] By the time Americans reach the age of eighteen, they have watched television for more hours than they have attended school. Almost all (98 percent) American homes have television sets, and half the homes have two sets, which are in use six or seven hours a day. But though they are bombarded with information, Americans seem to have limited capacity for absorbing information vital to the future of their country. The decaying infrastructure of the country; poverty and homelessness; the pollution of air, ground, and seas; the national debt; widespread and well-known mismanagement, fraud, and theft in military spending—these are problems that need to be dealt with but do not appear to figure significantly in the awareness of voters. Why not? Consider the issue of poverty.

The problems of the poor do not become issues for the middle-class majority in part because of lack of awareness or repression from consciousness. Philip Slater has called it the "Toilet Assumption": Offensive matters are flushed away, kept out of sight, and so are invisible to the majority of Americans.[7] In earlier times that was impossible; slops thrown out the second-story window were plainly in view; beggars, old people, eccentrics were seen and known, tolerated and cared for. But with the advent of specialized institutions, general affluence, and central highways, it has become easy to ignore and avoid the problems of the "other America" of which Michael Harrington wrote.[8] The "invisible Americans," the poor, elderly, mentally ill, children, sick, black, unemployed, Appalachian mountaineers, were off the main track, out of sight and so out of mind. Television's sweeping but superficial coverage of the plight of such people has but a momentary impact. These problems are sufficiently severe, widespread, and enduring, however, that they are periodically rediscovered in America. The question is whether citizens will mobilize and hold their elected officials accountable for action on behalf of the poor. Is the citizen who is related to his or her world through the television set prepared to act in the public realm?

The Citizen as Spectator

The view of citizenship held by the ancient Greeks throws into bold relief what we have lost, or are in danger of losing, in the transformation of citizen into television viewer. In the classical view of citizenship, as interpreted by Hannah Arendt, the public realm is the space in which people appear to one another in order to act and to speak together. In words compressing large meanings into brief compass, she writes: "Man's inability to rely upon himself or to have complete faith in himself (which is the same thing) is the price human beings pay for freedom; and the impossibility of remaining unique masters of what they do, of knowing its consequences and relying upon the future, is the price they pay for plurality and reality, for the joy of inhabiting together with others a world whose reality is guaranteed for each by the presence of all."[9] This complex and richly suggestive statement may not be comprehensible by the citizen as television viewer, and for several reasons. First, it is highly unlikely that a sentence as long as this and containing as many ideas, interrelated and subtle in their connotations, was ever spoken on television. But beyond that, television as a medium disposes one not to make the effort to plumb the meaning of such a statement. It may even render one incapable of understanding the ideas. Third, this view of citizenship and what it entails may appear to be so much at odds with political reality as to be dismissed as an unrealistic and undesirable standard of citizenship. At the least, it will serve as a critical vantage point from which to assess the shift from knowledge to information and the transformation of citizen into consumer and spectator.

"Politics," said Ronald Reagan in 1966, "is just like show business."[10] It might seem that the movie or television screen in contemporary American society is not so different from the dramatic presentation of public man in eighteenth-century London or even of the theater in ancient Athens, which was for the citizen the most appropriate mirror of the heroic deeds of public man. In fact, however, the differences are critical. The Greek and the Englishman participated directly or vicariously in a public drama that had vital connections with their lives. Whether deeds were noble and glorious or base and infamous, they were *public,* they had to do with common enterprises and purposes. Television is addressed to the single individual as spectator and consumer. The television viewer is not part of a visible audience but shut up in his or her own room. One does not participate in a communal response to what is enacted. In the darkened movie theater and alone before the television set, the lack of interaction either with what is on the screen or with an audience can produce a feeling of emptiness. The role of spectator of "reality," rather than of participant in the public realm, is exacerbated by the fact that before the television set one is a consumer.

The television commercial has become the fundamental metaphor for political discourse, says Neil Postman.[11] That was reflected in the title of Joe McGinnis's book about the campaign of Richard Nixon in 1968, *The Selling of the President.* Appearance is what counts in the advertisement. The commercial is a series of images condensed into sixty seconds or less. It promises instant therapy. The politics of imagery leads voters to look for immediate solutions, simple answers to complex problems. The commercial appeals to the viewer's "self-interest," but this has little to do with genuine interests such as productive work, more effective political representation of voters' interests, and improvement of public amenities. The commercial is calculated to make viewers feel better and to indulge themselves, to enjoy symbolic satisfactions rather than attain concrete interests. Politics also tends to focus on the symbolic rather than the real interests of citizens.

In their obsession with image and instancy, commercial and political discourse alike provide no historical context by which information can be understood. But without a context, facts are either meaningless or can be given any meaning desired. Hence we have more "facts," more "information," than ever, and less shared public understanding of the truth. This is due both to the lack of historical context and to the passivity of the spectator-consumer audience. Information becomes entertainment, and so do politics, religion, and education.

The Citizen as Consumer

If, as former Federal Communication Commissioner Nicholas Johnson has said, "television is an extension of our consciousness,"[12] how do we experience ourselves on the screen? We see ourselves as greedy players on the game shows, voyeurs of soap opera debaucheries, and insatiable addicts of sex and violence. In smaller blips, commercials glorify the good life: effortless, odorless, pleasure filled, pain free, beautiful to behold, and possible to attain—all the allurements directed to the passive spectator in front of the screen. The appeal is to consumer, not the citizen. The consumer is a master image that helps explain the decline of public life.

The values embedded in television culture are not new. Consumerism is a combination of individualism and materialism, values that in the American moral tradition have strongly influenced the political ideals of liberty and equality. Indeed, according to the historian Daniel Boorstin,[13] the story of the "democratic experience" from the Civil War to the present can be described most aptly as participation in the consumer society. It is a colorful story, but as a synonym for democracy it leaves something to be desired. It reduces public life to marketplace transactions and satisfactions; it ignores other values essential to personal and civic life; and it excludes millions of American citizens from full participation in the democratic experience.

Even if we were satisfied with the equation of consumerism and democracy, we would have to face the fact that many are excluded from that version of democracy and the good life. There is a tremendous life gap between the rhetoric of equality of opportunity and the realities of American society. To line up at the starting line in the race for jobs, security, and affluence means little if one is handicapped with a broken leg. While legally sanctioned forms of racial discrimination have been largely eliminated, equality of opportunity remains a cruel dream for those unable to compete because of disabilities and deprivation.

The marketplace makes no distinction between the world of goods and the good world. The basis for qualitative judgment must be found elsewhere than in quantitative transactions. Qualitative judgments about the good life are necessary for a good society. The easy equation of the good life with material goods, the dominance of the commercial over the moral imagination, is being challenged by the threat of ecological disaster. That growing threat may be the only force powerful enough to make us aware of what is lost in the process of making a world of goods. Without some critical vantage point from which to assess the images and allurements of the world of goods conveyed by television, the viewer lacks the ability to transcend his or her identity as consumer. Even before one asks What is my personal relation to what I see and hear? it is necessary to ask Who am I?

Who Am I?

I am the owner of a house, two cars, two television sets, a VCR, a word processor, and an accumulation of things in the basement that I must have wanted at one time or another. I am a consumer. I am also a son or daughter, wife or husband, parent; a student or lawyer or service station manager or office worker; a member of a church or synagogue; a block leader for recycling in my community, a secretary of the League of Women Voters, a fan of the Chicago Bulls, a Democrat or Republican. In my fantasy life I am a future Joe DiMaggio or Martina Navratilova, another Martin Luther King, Jr., or President of the United States. I have many shifting, tenuous, and fragile identities, informed by the media, Hollywood, advertising. Who am I?

Hollywood has an answer. The first Hollywood actor to become President of the United States spoke from the White House on the occasion of the 1981 Academy Awards. "Film is forever," said President Reagan. "It is the motion picture that shows all of us not only how we look and sound but—more important—how we feel."[14] If movies and television tell us—or "show all of us"—who we are, we are indeed the creatures of the corporate advertiser. What consumer would dare question his creator? Only a citizen could do that.

How can I distinguish myself from the identities foisted on me by the commercial culture? After all, *identity* is a psychosocial concept, a function of my interaction with my communities. The construction of my identity is not altogether of my own doing—for consider the most personal thing about me, my name, conferred on me by others. But understanding the identity given me by parents, community, culture, media, is one thing; choosing what I will be is quite another. I must choose who I am and who I shall be—but how to do that without some independent footing, some leverage point from which to assess the multifarious images? I can respond to the ethical question only if I have sufficient "ego strength," security in my own identity, to exercise discernment and critical judgment in reading the news and watching television. But how to do that when television itself confers our identity on us?

The authors of a recent study concluded that sex education classes have little effect on adolescents' sexual habits. "A classroom course alone," they said, "cannot be expected to change sexual behavior in a direction that is in opposition to the adolescent's sexual world as molded by the television, motion picture, music and advertising industries, as well as peer group and adult role models."[15] They observed that sex education programs have been effective where efforts to lower the teen pregnancy rate have included parents, media, and the community as a whole.

Fortunately, even in the information age, the primary agents in development of personality are not movies, television, and advertisers. Identity is forged in social interaction, beginning with our families. How one thinks of oneself is the mirror image of how one thinks of others. If I accept for myself the role of spectator and consumer, I will see others as objects. If I know myself to be person-in-community and citizen of a commonwealth, I will see others as free and equal, that is, fellow beings whose dignity and worth I respect, to whom I have obligations and on whom I rely for much that I need. To know myself as more than the cultural images that would define me, I require anchorage in the real world of human relations. Knowledge of self comes not through introspection or scientific investigation but in locating myself in the place from which I come, my history, my own story.

We do not spend much time reflecting on who we are. Routines, habits, unconscious patterns of behavior get us through the day with a minimum of reflection. We do not pause to ask ourselves which shoelace to tie first. We fix breakfast, eat, go to school or drive to work, and negotiate our daily lives for the most part without asking ourselves, Who am I? It attracts our attention when we find a person who persists in plumbing the depths of his or her own history and who arrives at an understanding of himself or herself that somehow impinges on our own lives. The poet, novelist, and farmer Wendell Berry gives us such an account.

Recovering the Self

As a grown man, Wendell Berry knew that he carried within him a "hidden wound," a malignant heritage of racism. He had a general knowledge of it, as he had a general knowledge of his own life. But it was not until he faced it and began to re-collect the memories of his early life that he was able to sort through them in order to lay bare the wound for healing. In seeking the roots of his own life, he recovered himself and gave us a powerful statement of a man's personal relationship to what he knows.[16]

When after several years of living in various places Berry returned to Kentucky, he bought a small farm near where he had grown up and reestablished connections with his native place. To find his own truth, he probed his memories of Nick Watkins and Aunt Georgie, two black persons whom he knew and loved as a boy. He was not interested in assuaging his guilt or in musing on what might have been but for the blight of racism. He knew that in his memories of these two people and in his allegiance to them, he had a moral resource that was vital to his development as a person.

Berry found that the fact that his own family had once owned slaves implicated him in a painful history. In reflecting on the story about a slave whom his great-grandfather sold and who was mistreated by the new slaveowner, he began to trace the connections between slavery and a culture that had to deny to itself the evil of the institution. He found a silence in the language, a silence that was the shape of the black man. The language of the lifeworld of home and family, farm and town, work and recreation, might express the bondage of black to white, but the public language had no words for slavery. It hid the anguish of racism in euphemistic words, the brutality of a whole social system in guarded, polite language of gentility and chivalry.

The white man's alienation from the land Berry traces to the landowner's relegation of hard manual labor to "nigger work." The black servant has had an immediate, direct, and concrete relation to the land, whereas the white landowner has had an abstract role, concerned with making money from it. Money was the dominant feature of the white society Berry knew as a child. It was money that drew people off the farm and away from established communities. Money determined what was rational, what counted for success, and what one had to do to get to the top. As a result, he says, "We knew and took for granted: marriage without love; sex without joy; drink without conviviality; birth, celebration, and death without adequate ceremony; faith without doubt or trial; belief without deeds; manners without generosity; 'good English' without exact speech, without honesty, without literacy."[17] In contrast to this artificial society, Nick and Aunt Georgie exemplify the history of a people who learned how to endure and survive, and who developed an authentic culture based in work and expressed in a music of their own. "In the course of their long ordeal," observes Berry, "[they] have developed—as white society has *not*—the understanding and the means both of small private pleasures and of communal grief and celebration and joy."[18]

In withholding responsibility for the land from the black man and by cutting himself off from closeness to the land by the black man's labor, the white man has deprived himself of needed wisdom. Lacking a sense of dependence on the land and responsibility for it, city dwellers have no rituals and celebrations that keep alive the consciousness of their relationships to each other and to the earth. Berry sees in this the roots of ecological disaster.

American society is today deeply divided by racism. College campuses, desegregated but not integrated, reflect the problem. The division is more than racial, it is psychological and moral, within as well as between ourselves. In hiding the truth of our racism from ourselves we have repressed our history and sealed off a part of ourselves. We can come to know the truth that can set us free only by coming to know each other, blacks and whites. If we are to find healing for the hidden wound of racism and regain a healthy relation to the world around us, we would do well to learn from the American Indian of 350 years ago. His respect for the earth on which he knew himself to be dependent, his reverence for the sky and practice of self-restraint and balance in his relationships, have much to teach us. Our wholeness as a people awaits the restoration of our relationships between blacks and whites and reds. Wendell Berry concludes his story: "As soon as we have fulfilled the hollow in our culture, the silence in our speech, with the fully realized humanity of the black man—and it follows, of the American Indian—then there will appear over the horizon of our consciousness another figure as well: that of the American white man, our *own* humanity, lost to us these three and a half centuries, the time of all our life on this continent."[19] This is a recognition that we need the knowledge of others, our life is incomplete apart from theirs, our destinies are bound together.

What Is My Personal Relation to What I Don't Know?

What I do *not* know about the social, economic, and political realities of life in America and in other countries is a function of my ignorance of the stories of others. "The American story" is in fact a selective tale that incorporates what is of value and interest to some citizens but excludes others. There are some things we cannot know unless we listen to the stories of others. Some college students discover this when they spend a summer working with the homeless. Male-dominated law faculties are being awakened by women lawyers to the inequality and sexism inherent in Western law. These feminist lawyers are effecting changes in a wide range of legal issues, such as sexual harassment in the workplace, protection of pregnant working women, and equal treatment. Professor Martha Minow of Harvard Law School has said: "The lively response to feminist legal work confirms its power and its indelible message that those who have been excluded have something important to say."[20] Feminist activists working with battered women may have some knowledge that the research of professionals involved in hierarchical bureaucratic structures does not contain. One writer observes: "By helping the victim to place her individual suffering within a wider social and political framework, activists set the stage for possible shifts in self-perception: the once-victim can work to transform a situation that damages her, unlike the welfare client locked into static dependency on agencies and experts."[21]

The middle-class American has little sense of what it means to be powerless. A friend of mine got some inkling of it when she was a helper in a day-care center, making $3.45 an hour. Pat saw the director take a child who had misbehaved into the "black room" for discipline. The child screamed that she was afraid of the dark. Pat went to the door and opened it enough to say to the director that she would hold the child in her arms until the mother could get there. The director was furious and, when they talked about the incident later, told Pat that what she had done was wrong by every rule in the code book. Pat said that it was not right to treat the child like that and that she could not just stand by in such a case. The director said she had no business opening her mouth because she was "a worker." Pat replied that she had taken the job to help out, that she was doing it while finishing her graduate work, and that her husband was a professor at the university. She did not have to work and did not intend to work under those circumstances. The director immediately backed off and became "reasonable."

It is difficult for the reader of this book, as it is for me, to understand the worker's sense of powerlessness until one experiences it. But there is another side to the incident just described. That is the sudden discovery of the power one possesses because of one's economic and social class. The day-care helper became powerful at the point where she confronted the director and "blew the whistle." She would have been helpless had she not been intelligent, educated, and articulate. That was not enough, however.

She had connections with a community beyond the workplace. There were others to whom she could appeal, knowing that they would share her outrage at mistreatment of the weak and would be ready to act.

At a moment like that, one becomes aware not simply of the vulnerability of the powerless but also of the way in which power is a function of class structure. The day-care helper was a worker. She was not, however, dependent on her work or her employer for her livelihood. She had control over her own work life in direct proportion to her economic independence. She had power in correcting the abuse of the child to the degree that she had access to countervailing power beyond the workplace.

Education in America does not prepare students to assume responsibility for the plight of the weak and powerless in the society. It tends to socialize one into unquestioning acceptance of the status quo, partly by inattention to the inequities that result from institutional arrangements and the way power is exercised and partly by justifying the existing system in the name of the traditional American values of liberty, equality, property, and religion. Because these values are interpreted largely in terms of economic individualism, they do not function very well as critical standards for the evaluation of public policy. Issues such as health care, assistance to single mothers, and health and safety in the workplace can be adequately addressed only in the context of community.

A communal approach is required for the realization of the values of liberty and equality, in two respects. First, only in community is genuine liberty to be achieved. Our cherished human rights are ours only as long as there is a community ready to guarantee and protect them. Freedom is not simply the absence of oppression by others, it is the ability to exercise one's powers and to achieve one's potential as a creative and productive person. It is the opportunity to actualize and express oneself as a free and equal citizen in the civil community. Achievement of such liberty depends on nurture, care, and stimulus in a conducive environment, which a free society should seek to provide for all. Second, liberty and equality for all depend for their realization on a community of citizens who will act on behalf of the needy, the outsiders, the abused, and the helpless. Liberty and equality will not be honored or sought in a society of individuals who assume that the common good will be achieved simply by individuals pursuing their own economic gain in the marketplace.

The Aim of Policy: A Flourishing Life

Each of us desires well-being. We wish to live a flourishing life. It is likely that some notion of the good life underlies most public policies and, for that matter, our fundamental conception of government. Such an ideal is, in fact, stated in the Declaration of Independence and elaborated in the Preamble to the Constitution. The Declaration declares that "all men ... are endowed by their Creator with certain unalienable rights ... among [which] are life, liberty, and the pursuit of happiness." The aims of government, according to the Constitution, are to "establish justice, insure domestic tranquillity, provide for the common defense, promote the general welfare and secure the blessings of liberty to ourselves and our posterity." The "general welfare" seems to refer to economic prosperity, but the "pursuit of happiness" must encompass more than economic well-being.

The pursuit of happiness, in the view of the Declaration, is the chief end of life to which all other rights and goods are means. This all-embracing goal of the citizen's life is a common good, which government, according to Declaration and Constitution, is designed to foster. For this reason, serious consideration needs to be given to the idea of the pursuit of happiness. If conceived in merely psychological terms, as the satisfaction of desires, the pursuit of happiness could not be the aim of government, for individual desires may clash with the rights of others. Understood in the more inclusive ethical sense, however, happiness is "a whole life enriched by the cumulative possession of all the goods that human beings rightly desire because they are naturally needed."[22] The pursuit of happiness in this sense is not simply an individualistic right but a common good that requires conditions that a society must provide for the sake of all its members. This was somewhat humorously illustrated recently when the evening news showed residents in one of the wealthiest communities in the country demonstrating against a new airport. Jets flying overhead were disrupting cocktail conversation and violating the quiet that millions of dollars can no longer buy. Freedom from noise for the wealthy and freedom from hunger for the destitute, as well as other conditions necessary for the flourishing life, are aims that are appropriate to public policy. Public policy rightly guarantees to all citizens those goods necessary for the pursuit of happiness, goods attained not by competition but by cooperation. They are the rights of all, to be pursued together.

This view of the flourishing life is not merely theoretical. It is a necessary vantage point for the ethical evaluation of public policy. Policy for the aging is a good example, particularly in the light of the fact that intergenerational competition for societal resources is becoming an urgent political issue. A syndicated columnist recently evoked some heated responses to an article in which she wrote about the economic gap opening up between those who own their own homes and those who do not.[23] This gap is frequently a generational one, for as real estate values of homeowners increase, many young would-be buyers find the cost of houses prohibitively high. The elderly as a group are becoming more prosperous relative to other age groups. With the growth of the aging population, the elderly constitute a powerful political lobby on behalf of their interests. But there are signs of a political backlash. As many of the elderly cried out against the increased costs of the catastrophic health insurance passed by Congress in 1988, there were expressions by others that government was already providing disproportionate benefits for the elderly. One health analyst was quoted as saying, "There's a strong undercurrent that the elderly are greedy geezers and it's someone else's turn [to receive benefits]."[24] Public policy is often one-sided—whatever the merits in this case—because of a failure to take a broad enough view. Aging policy needs to be considered within the framework of the life cycle as a whole, in terms of the inclusive community, and in view of the question of what it means to live a flourishing life.

A Test Case: Aging Policy

It is surprising that as the state of the elderly has improved over the past two decades, the public has perceived that condition as worsening. Two-thirds of those polled in a 1985 survey by the *Los Angeles Times* thought that poverty among the old was increasing, a view contradicted by the facts.[25] This pessimistic view of aging is caused in part by the very success of biomedical technology in keeping elderly patients alive longer than ever before. As more and more people live longer, many find that the last stage of life is one that inspires anxiety and dread rather than contentment. Though many of the elderly are better off than ever, the cost of health care for the old is expected to rise from the $80 billion of federal and private money spent in 1981 to an expected $200 billion (in 1980 dollars) by the year 2000. Daniel Callahan notes several complaints over this rise in health costs. First, is it fair and reasonable that so much more public funds should go to the elderly rather than to benefits for children? Second, is it wise—and humane—to spend so much of that money for the care of the elderly dying? Third, should such a large proportion of health-care research and technology be devoted to conditions affecting the elderly more than other age groups?[26]

The conflict over these issues could lead to intergenerational warfare in a "zero-sum" society in which even those who gain at the expense of others are in danger of losing ground. The politics of interest-group pluralism can offer no solution to this problem. Traditional welfare policy is inadequate, as Harry R. Moody points out.[27] Liberals have pictured the elderly as the deserving poor, and because conservatives have seen their needs as legitimate, they have been willing to give the elderly public benefits denied to other groups. Policy has addressed the deficits and needs of old people without taking into account the strengths that might enable the old to help themselves and one another. Social policies in the United States have treated the elderly as consumers, not as contributing members of the society.

To correct the deficiencies of welfare policy, Moody proposes a "prodevelopmentalist" approach to aging policy.[28]

Moody's approach would try to reduce unnecessary dependency, while cultivating latent strengths; it would recognize the significant noneconomic contributions of voluntarism and self-help; and it would envision lifelong learning as a way of fostering the development of human capacities and social productivity. Such an approach would be more responsive to the needs and desires of the elderly, more supportive, and more economical than traditional policy.

An experiment demonstrates in a dramatic way the difference between a prodevelopmentalist approach and one that reinforces dependency. Nursing home residents were divided into two groups. In one group, the residents were given plants to care for. They were also allowed to choose the way they would spend their recreation time. The other group was told that the staff would take care of the plants placed in their rooms, and the residents were put in a preplanned recreational program. At the end of six months the group exercising responsible choice over their environment was healthier and had lost fewer members in death than the group that was a passive recipient of directions and service.[29]

Self-esteem, critical to the quality of life in any age, is weakened by social welfare interventions that create or encourage dependency. A prodevelopmental approach to policy will support institutional arrangements that sustain mutual self-help groups. It will develop programs for retraining older workers; educate the elderly in coping skills; and foster programs of education for leisure time and retirement. It will also educate for citizen participation in ways that go beyond the interest group that limits itself to its narrowly defined needs.[30] Instead of tolerating a division of the life cycle into a youth phase of education, an adult time of work, and an old age of enforced leisure, with a resulting lack of unity and meaning in life as a whole, such a view would take a unified view of life. It would keep policy from being skewed toward one age group to the neglect of another and would focus on social networks, supporting arrangements that would strengthen and enhance the life of all. In an affluent society that nevertheless faces critical choices in how resources are to be allocated, this is an approach to policy that is humane and realistic.

An Emerging Perspective on Public Policy

The prodevelopmentalist approach to aging policy illustrates an emerging new policy perspective. Those taking this view see serious limitations to the "hard path" of high-technology medicine, which is focused on disease, based in large medical centers, and geared to acute care and prolongation of life through heroic measures. They urge the "soft path," which stresses prevention of disease and promotion of health, encourages self-help, and takes a bottom-up approach to social policy, as in hospice, home health care, and mutual-aid groups. The soft path, says Harry Moody, "would have lower costs, be more stable, and be more flexible in its use of biotechnology for chronic illnesses."[31] He acknowledges that the feasibility of the soft path depends on sizable social investment in such things as health education and promotion, which is lacking today.

What Moody describes as the soft path of development accords with the new paradigm of health care that many see emerging. This new paradigm (conceptual framework) finds the biomedical model of health, based on the worldview of Newton and Descartes, to be outmoded. The Newtonian and Cartesian worldview was a mathematical and mechanistic view of nature, in which physical phenomena were reduced to motion caused by the mutual attraction of material particles.[32] Methodological reductionism, dualism, and mechanism have continued to characterize medical science, which is still based, in the words of George Engel, on "the notion of the body as a machine, of disease as a consequence of breakdown of the machine, and of the doctor's task as repair of the machine."[33] The biomedical model, with its objective, impersonal, and technological treatment of the diseased body, is challenged by the "second medical revolution," which promotes a holistic, behavioral, and environmental approach to health care. The new paradigm broadens the concern with the body to include the whole person, who interacts with complex social and ecological structures. Instead of the focus of scientific medicine on bacteria and virus, neoplasms, and vascular plaques, the new approach includes as a part of diagnosis and treatment negative attitudes, dysfunctional images, and life-change events that produce social alienation, along with automated workplace and sedentary lifestyles.[34]

Scientific medicine based on the biomedical model raises unrealistic hopes for technological cures, even as it escalates the costs of medical treatment beyond the capacity of the society to pay. Even though health expenditures cost more than 11 percent of our gross national product, America does not fare well in comparison to other countries: "During the recent period of rapidly rising consumption of medical services, the United States ranked eighteenth in the world in life expectancy from birth; although the life-span continues to rise, the United States has nevertheless fallen among the modernized nations of the world, and now lags behind such countries as Greece, Spain, and Italy, countries whose per-capita health expenditures are a fraction of ours."[35] Illness and disability among the young are increasing.

The vicious cycle will not be broken until we take a communal and ecological perspective on the health of human beings. President Derek Bok of Harvard University pointed the way when he called on Harvard Medical School to take as its goal the need "to understand the emotional, psychological and cultural underpinnings of human behavior, including the interweaving of mind and body in health."[36]

Though Americans are beginning to allocate funds to treat toxic elements in the physical environment, they spend little on housing the homeless, teaching the illiterate, and creating pleasant conditions for the disabled and elderly. Social conditions are as responsible for human misery as disease itself. Rape, for example, is the fastest growing of violent crimes. According to current estimate, one in six women will suffer rape during her life. "We must recognize these events," says Leonard Sagan, "as being just as much public health problems as are smallpox epidemics." [37]

The Community Approach to Public Policy

The prodevelopmentalist, ecological approach of person-in-community represents the perspective of a growing number concerned with public life and public policy. This shared perspective is a function of the moral imagination, for it discerns possibilities for creative social change in seeing the political situation in a new way. It perceives persons as essentially related to one another in moral community. It takes account of self-interest but apprehends as well the higher realism of personal and common good that can be achieved only in cooperative vision and effort. It recognizes that action begins with the individual person and that in taking responsibility for oneself as a member of inclusive community, one sets in motion creative forces for social change. This may indeed be visionary—it has to be, in order to transcend the entrenched myth of atomistic individualism—but it is also practical. It can be applied to problems such as hate crimes, illiteracy, and AIDS.

Conventional approaches have not been very effective in resolving the problem of hate crimes. Congress has enacted legislation requiring the attorney general to compile data on hate crimes, which include assault, harassment, or intimidation due to a person's race, ethnic background, sexual preference, or religion. In one city, the police chief has achieved some success in dealing with hate crimes with the use of unorthodox tactics. In one instance, a white man turned the antique cannon in his front yard toward the living room of the black family that had moved next door. When an officer asked him to remove it, he refused. Officers then went to see the people and businesses in the neighborhood, asking whether they thought the man's action improved the value of their property and reputation and whether it reflected their own ethical standards. When neighbors called on the black family and spoke to the owner of the cannon, it was removed. "A cross burning is not a simple arson, and a swastika painted on a temple is not mere vandalism," said Chief Neil J. Behan, of the Baltimore County Police Department, who handled the incident. "I tell my officers that they are not to leave a neighborhood after a hate crime until that victim and neighborhood are made whole again."[38]

The problem of illiteracy in the United States is growing. In a study conducted for the Department of Education in 1975, 23 million adults in this country were found to be functionally illiterate. In a recent California survey, it was found that 25 percent of adult Californians were functionally illiterate; the number is increasing by 230,000 per year. Estimated costs of this burden in unemployment, welfare, and prison expenses are a billion dollars a year.[39] A preventive strategy is needed. There is a model at hand. One of the best-known intervention programs designed to help culturally disadvantaged children was Head Start. It was designed to compensate deprived preschool children with the kind of education other children receive within the family. In early evaluation of the programs it was found that the children's initial intellectual improvement declined after several years. In more recent reevaluation studies, however, it was found that as these same children reached high school, there was less delinquency, lower dropout and pregnancy rates, with twice the employment and educational training rates of those seen among the controls. There was, in fact, a 50 percent improvement.[40]

A communal approach to the problem of AIDS is called for if both individual liberty and the common good are to be preserved. A study prepared for the World Health Organization released in May 1989 predicted that the global number of AIDS cases would increase by tenfold by the year 2000, rising from 450,000 in 1989 to 5 million.[41] Reactions to the AIDS epidemic illustrate the attitude, widespread from medieval times to modernity, that has advocated quarantine as a means of protecting the community by isolating those afflicted by epidemics. This attitude has been reinforced by legal moralism, which has used the law to protect the morality of the community by punishing moral deviance. As recently as 1978, Justice William Rehnquist argued that the question of constitutionality of laws controlling the free association of homosexual students on college campuses is like the question "whether those suffering from measles have a constitutional right, in violation of quarantine regulations, to associate together and with others who do not presently have measles."[42] It may be that AIDS will force our society to recognize the injustice of treating a minority as less than human and to ensure equality in fundamental civil rights. As AIDS teaches us that we are all responsible for one another, for educating ourselves, for demonstrating compassion, and for protecting the privacy and dignity of all persons, Americans may recognize the need to adopt a program of national health insurance for all citizens.

An ethical perspective on public policy emerging out of our experience of community, including conflicts of interest within it and threats to its well-being (such as AIDS), will have three essential features. It will attempt to see the issue whole, within broad contexts of meaning that include value traditions and critical reflection on those values. It will include the whole community, in which everyone counts. It will give special weight to the public good and to the needs of the poor, the needy, and the marginal. Such a perspective will be shared by actors in the public realm, free and equal citizens who hold one another accountable for what they know.

The Religious Factor

Throughout this book, religion has for the most part remained in the background. This is because faith is a personal matter. Yet it must be included in the consideration of the relation of citizen to public life, not for philosophical reasons but because churches and synagogues figure in American life in ways too important to ignore. The significance of American religion for social ethics is best grasped by focusing on particular religious communities, rather than on such a nebulous entity as civil religion. As a basis for a social ethic, civil religion is too artificial and contrived, too prone to ideological manipulation and too identified with mainstream Protestantism to the neglect or exclusion of religious and ethnic minorities. The historian Martin Marty proposes the notion of the "public church" as an idea that better accords with the realities of American religion and the pluralistic character of political life. "The public church," declares Marty, "is a communion of communions, each of which lives its life partly in response to its separate tradition and partly to the call for a common Christian vocation."[43]

Alexis de Tocqueville spoke of the need for sacrifice and "instinctive public virtues," and saw religion as an indispensable force in inculcating obligations to others and in restraining cupidity and self-interest. A political religion harnessed to the purposes of government was strongly opposed by Tocqueville, but he rejected equally a purely private morality. Public virtues were needed, but Christianity with its achievement of a human community without national boundaries had failed to define and inculcate the duties of citizens to their country. The nature of the commercial society with its materialistic individualism, the eclipse of quality by quantity, and the leveling tendencies in intellectual life caused Tocqueville to fear the loss of public virtue. A vigorous democratic society required natural resources, laws, and, above all, mores, the moral habits of mind and temper that would infuse and legitimate the laws. And for this, religion was essential. With its reference to transcendent reason and justice and to an inclusive humanity, it was a bulwark against the "tyranny of the majority" and the power of a central government. It also tempered the individualism of Americans with its ethos of community of church, nation, and mankind.

With a historical tradition antedating the rise of the liberal state, the religious community can question such cultural value assumptions as economic individualism when they are allowed to eclipse other, more humane values. It judges the self-centered life of materialism with images and experience of life together in which persons care for and share with one another. It evaluates excessive wants in the light of urgent human needs. It affirms a context of meaning and value in which the individual can find fulfillment in relation to family, work, and community. It provides a vision of a just and inclusive human community and a critical perspective on all political ideologies. As the historian Herbert Butterfield has said: "The Christian is particularly called to carry his thinking outside that framework which a nation or a political party or a social system or an accepted regime or a mundane theology provides. Even the preservation of what we may love as the existing order of things—even Anglo-Saxon ideals and western values—are not the absolute values for the Christian."[44] The religious community is only one community within the civil society. But it bears witness to the fact of community and to civil society as a community of communities, a communal society.

Religious communities inspire and nourish visions of the good society. However muted or sporadic may be their expression, the ideals of justice and the common good are too much embedded in the historical identity of churches and synagogues and their sacred texts to be ignored or compromised for long. The church may be a particular community prone to becoming an in-group, but its self-centeredness is subject to continued challenge by its biblical and theological norms. It bears witness to a communal society whose members give special consideration to the weakest and neediest among them, who are just and fair in the treatment of all, and who seek to live in harmony and peace within the larger community of nations. It can help rekindle "the loss of *civitas*, that spontaneous willingness to obey the law, to respect the right of others, to forgo the temptations of private enrichment at the expense of the public weal."[45] In varying degrees, religious communities keep alive the calling to social service, stewardship of means, and civic responsibility.

Churches as Public Interest Groups

Churches and other religious groups have exerted a powerful force in national politics, notably during the revolutionary period in sermonizing and pamphleteering for liberty, in the Abolitionist struggle to free the slaves, in the response of Protestantism's social gospel to the economic and social problems spawned by the Industrial Revolution, and in the civil rights movement led by Martin Luther King, Jr. Today the National Council of Churches, the World Council of Churches, the National Conference of Christians and Jews, and denominational and other religious groups monitor with a close eye the whole range of policy issues in an effort to keep citizens informed and to mobilize them for action.

Churches participate in various ways in the political process as interest groups. They exert influence and pressure through their media centers, lobbying in Washington, and joint efforts with other religious and secular groups. One such example is the United Methodist Church, which through its General Board of Church and Society attempts to provide "forthright witness on social issues" across a wide spectrum of American life. In one year this included the monitoring of compliance with the World Health Organization code by the Nestlé Foods Corporation, Abbott Laboratories, Bristol Meyers, and American Home Products; hearings, advocacy, and networking on agricultural and rural life issues; a Consultation on Pornography; organizing citizens for passage of legislation on acid rain; and planning several conferences on family issues in conjunction with other national groups.[46] Because of their long tradition of theological and ethical inquiry, church groups can bring a broad historical perspective and a richly informed judgment to bear on public issues. They are most effective in delineating the moral aspects of such issues and in seeking to discern general principles relevant to those issues.

A development of major significance in the past twenty years is the establishment of a number of centers for the study of ethics and public policy throughout the country, probably the most influential being the Hastings Center, the location of the Institute of Society, Ethics and the Life Sciences.[47] In colloquia, research, and education, these centers bring together religious and secular specialists in biomedical ethics and other issues to focus on problems of biomedical, social science, professional and political ethics. It is now normal practice for theologians and philosophical ethicists to be included on national commissions, making recommendations on such issues as genetic engineering research.[48]

Getting Involved

If I am moved to participate in the public realm, where do I start? Perhaps the place to begin is with a reading of the news. Rather than raise the ethical question after the experts have defined the facts, I will make my own judgments. I will try to discern what the information means, whose interest it serves, and what and who are left out of the news.

To read the news in order to find out what is going on here, I need to have some touchstones of reality. What *dis*interested (not *un*interested) persons and groups can throw light on the issue or situation? For this, I need to look to groups and persons I can trust. What's in it for them? Are they acting out of narrow self-interest? Not so likely if the group is the League of Women Voters, Common Cause, Amnesty International, Witness for Peace, the Prison and Jail Project, Habitat for Humanity, the Center for Defense Information, or many other public interest groups. Public interest groups may sometimes act like other special-interest groups in their lobbying efforts, failing to get all the relevant facts and presenting a one-sided view. But they are advocates for those in need, for the environment, for more honest and efficient government, for liberty, justice, and the common good. Because they are acting out of broad interest and concern for the public good, they are more likely to be trusted, and for good reason.

It is time to return to the student vigil for a moment. It brings us back to "the process and the people," as one of the participants put it during the 1988 reunion. The bond of community forged in that experience has kept some of the vigilites true to a kind of vocation. As articulate as they are, many find it difficult to say exactly what it is that gives them their certain angle on public life. But there it is. In some real sense, there is continuity with the lives of a group of social activists on the Duke campus today. One spends a summer working with the homeless in Harlem and comes back to campus to lead efforts, at last successful, to get the administration to invest in low-cost housing for the poor in the local community. Another, a premedical student who does not think of himself as an activist, reflects on his responsibility for his own health and begins to trace his responsibility into the public sphere.

When a college student begins to see a moral connection between herself or himself and public life, it alters the meaning of education. One person believes his most important insight as a college student fifteen years ago was his realization that things might not be what they seem. He observes that some undergraduates are oriented to see new possibilities; others do not appear even to be aware of their responsibility to explore other possibilities. These are not idle musings. This man has gone to El Salvador to work on behalf of victims of forced military "recruitment," in which military personnel simply "conscript" young men, often under the legal draft age, from buses, streets, and rural areas, without informing their families. What leads a person like this to "get involved"?

Moral Imagination and Hope

A man does not suddenly leave the United States at age thirty-six to spend at least three years in Central America in work that is hazardous to his health without knowing who he is and what he is about. What motivates him? He has a sense of calling rooted in his family; in the lives of persons he has known, including those he has encountered in books; in his Christian faith; and in communities that have nurtured and supported him as he has followed the leads in his life for fifteen years. This sounds too simple, even too pat, as I try to sum up what he said. Something essential remains that cannot be pinned down. He acknowledges that his goals do not have the kind of clarity that those of his businessman father have. "Yours," he said to his father, "are twenty-year plans with five-year subplans, a corporate view of hierarchy and jobs. You have to have clarity about where you're going. I have goals too but not the same kind of clarity about what I'll be doing five years from now." A man like this has to have hope.

The person I just described strikes me as one of the most inner-directed people I have known. Yet he observes that he has always struggled with his vocation in some context of community, primarily the community of faith. He declares: "The image of the body of Christ is extremely important for me to have a sense of calling in my life—I don't have to do everything but I can depend on others." At a local gathering of Amnesty International, several people were talking about the plight of prisoners of conscience around the world. Toward the end of the conversation, one of them asked the visitor, Pat Derian, former assistant secretary of state for human rights in the Carter administration: "What keeps you going? How can you have hope?" She answered without hesitation: "I think of people I know who because of their work for human rights are in constant danger of their lives and the lives of their families. My work doesn't cost me much," she said. "My life is safe and secure. But they know what they do can cost their lives. They give me hope."

No rational argument, no matter how well buttressed by logical analysis and pertinent facts, will lead me to act as citizen in the public realm. Everything depends on what I own up to in terms of my personal knowledge and on what I see. The linked ideas we have pursued have a certain logic. At crucial moments, they may elicit the reader's sympathetic agreement. More compelling by far will be the lives of persons whom we know, or know about, who by some feat of sustained moral imagination manage to see beyond the marketplace and beyond narrow self-interest to a public realm in which citizens find their happiness in life together, in working to improve the quality of their lives and their environment, in talking with one another about things that matter in the long run.

The ethical question is the point of contact with reality, which is the ground of hope. Only if I am *connected* with what I know and value, connected with those I care for and trust, connected with the embracing and sustaining world, can I hope. Like the relational qualities of love, faith, and knowledge, *hope* characterizes the communal perspective. Hope, unlike optimism (which is essentially a cheery outlook on the future, without any necessary relation to reality), is intersubjective, personal, and communal. We hope together; hope is a function of human and social action, not of impersonal processes and trends. The technological mentality is congenitally optimistic, but it provides no basis for hope or despair. We hope because we can count on others, their competence and creativity, their loyalty and goodwill, their care and compassion. We hope because we are part of a community that finally knows no bounds and that is wreathed in a mystery whose meaning some see as infinite love.

In the first week of June 1989, an event occurred in the history of China that no one could have foretold. The Chinese government turned on its own people in an act of brutality that shocked the world. Following a massive military assault that wounded and killed unknown numbers of young people demonstrating for democracy in Tiananmen Square, Beijing, the people were stunned and in disarray. Tiananmen Square was virtually empty. Then the television camera caught an incredible sight. A young man stood alone in the path of the long line of tanks moving into the Square. As the tanks advanced, he stood his ground. When the tank in front of the line stopped, shifted its direction, and moved forward, he quickly moved to place himself in front of it. The tank paused, shifted, and faced the figure again. The young man tried to climb aboard the tank, but failed. He then stood before the immobilized tank until other youths rushed out and took him off. Just hours before, tanks had crushed the bodies of those in their way. Was this youth dazed and unaware of what he was doing? Was he momentarily insane? Was he, in cold fact, ready to die for the cause of democracy?

The image will not go away. It will surely take its place with other symbols in the history of the twentieth century that evoke the depths and heights of the human spirit: the bodies in the gas chambers of Auschwitz; the naked baby crying on the railroad tracks of Shanghai, surrounded with debris of the Japanese bombing; the half-robed figure of Mahatma Gandhi; the mushroom cloud of the first atomic bomb; the view of planet earth taken from the spaceship Apollo on the first moon voyage; the Vietnamese girl running down the street with arms outstretched, body on fire; Sheriff "Bull" Connor unleashing police dogs on black nonviolent protestors; Martin Luther King, Jr., leading the first civil rights march in Montgomery; a lone young man in Tiananmen Square, defying the forces massed to crush resisters. Framed in all this, what does our life mean? Despair and hope. But hope in despair, for the human face remains, calling for response from other human faces.

What I know of the twentieth century holds me hostage. I am personally responsible for the human future.

NOTES

Chapter 1. Public Policy and the Ethical Question

1. Thomas R. Dye, *Understanding Public Policy* (Englewood Cliffs, N.J.: Prentice-Hall, 1972), 3.

2. Duncan MacRae, Jr., and James A. Wilde, *Policy Analysis for Public Decisions* (Belmont, Calif.: Duxbury Press, 1979), 3.

3. David Easton, *The Political System* (New York: Knopf, 1953), 129.

4. Lewis A. Froman, Jr., "Public Policy," in *International Encyclopedia of the Social Sciences,* ed. David L. Sills (New York: Macmillan and Free Press, 1968), 13:204.

5. Charles E. Lindblom, *The Policy-Making Process,* 2d ed. (Englewood Cliffs, N.J.: Prentice-Hall, 1980), 2.

6. Charles E. Lindblom, "The Science of 'Muddling Through,'" *Public Administration Review* 19 (Spring 1959): 79–88; Lindblom, *Policy-Making Process,* pt. 1; Dye, *Understanding Public Policy,* chap. 2.

7. Lindblom, *The Policy-Making Process,* 1st ed. (Englewood Cliffs, N.J.: Prentice-Hall, 1968), 23.

8. Charles E. Lindblom, *Politics and Markets* (New York: Basic Books, 1977), 356.

9. For a recent treatment of these issues, see M.E. Hawkesworth, *Theoretical Issues in Policy Analysis* (Albany: State University of New York Press, 1988), esp. chap. 2, "Policy Analysis: Images and Issues."

10. Charles E. Lindblom and David Cohen, *Usable Knowledge: Social Science and Social Problem Solving* (New Haven: Yale University Press, 1979), 69, quoted in Hawkesworth, *Theoretical Issues,* 205.

11. See Dorothy Emmett, *Rules, Roles and Relations* (New York: Macmillan, 1966).

12. William K. Frankena, *Ethics* (Englewood Cliffs, N.J.: Prentice-Hall, 1963), 96. The view Frankena espouses here is set forth by Kurt Baier in *The Moral Point of View* (Ithaca, N.Y.: Cornell University Press, 1958).

13. See note 14.

14. See Stanley Hauerwas and Alasdair MacIntyre, eds., *Revisions: Changing Perspectives in Moral Philosophy* (Notre Dame, Ind.: University of Notre Dame Press, 1983), esp. Iris Murdoch, "Against Dryness: A Polemical Sketch," 43–50, and Ed-

mund Pincoffs, "Quandary Ethics," 92–112. See also Craig Dykstra, *Vision and Character, A Christian Educator's Alternative to Kohlberg* (New York: Paulist Press, 1981); David Burrell and Stanley Hauerwas, "From System to Story: An Alternative Pattern for Rationality in Ethics," in *The Roots of Ethics: Science, Religion, and Values,* ed. Daniel Callahan and H. Tristram Engelhardt, Jr. (New York: Plenum Press, 1981), 75–116; William F. May, *The Physician's Covenant* (Philadelphia: Westminster Press, 1983); Stephen Toulmin, "The Tyranny of Principles," *Hastings Center Report* 11, no. 6 (December 1981): 31–39.

15. Murdoch, "Against Dryness," 43.

16. This use of the word *usage* was suggested to me by William H. Poteat, who recalls getting the idea from an early essay by Ortega y Gassett. See William H. Poteat, *A Philosophical Daybook: Post-Critical Investigations* (Columbia: University of Missouri Press, 1990), 42, 93, 95.

17. Quoted in Donald N. McCloskey, *The Rhetoric of Economics* (Madison: University of Wisconsin Press, 1985), 29.

18. Michael J. Perry, *Morality, Politics, and Law, A Bicentennial Essay* (New York: Oxford University Press, 1988), 11; the last phrase, reminiscent of Aristotle, is the title of Reynolds Price's novel *A Long and Happy Life;* cf. John Rawls, *A Theory of Justice* (Cambridge, Mass.: Harvard University Press, 1971), 426.

19. See esp. the following works by Søren Kierkegaard: *Either/Or,* vol. 2 (Princeton: Princeton University Press, 1944); *Stages Upon Life's Way* (Princeton: Princeton University Press, 1940); *Fear and Trembling* (Princeton: Princeton University Press, 1945); and *The Sickness unto Death* (Princeton: Princeton University Press, 1941).

20. Abraham Kaplan, *American Ethics and Public Policy* (New York: Oxford University Press, 1966), 11.

21. Marjorie Grene, *The Knower and the Known* (London: Faber and Faber, 1966), 243; cf. 61.

22. There are antecedents for phrasing the ethical question as one of personal responsibility for knowledge, beginning with Socrates. Kierkegaard is the preeminent modern contributor to this tradition. Michael Polanyi developed a theory of personal knowledge in response to the twentieth-century challenges of Marxism and positivism. Others, Wittgenstein and Merleau-Ponty in particular, have also dealt with the presuppositions for ethical being and knowing in ways that bear importantly on the ethical question formulated in this way. See Michael Polanyi, *Personal Knowledge: Towards a Post-Critical Philosophy* (Chicago: University of Chicago Press, 1958); Ludwig Wittgenstein, *Philosophical Investigations,* trans. G.E.M. Anscombe, 3d ed. (New York: Macmillan, 1958); idem, *On Certainty,* ed. G.E.M. Anscombe and G.H. von Wright, trans. Denis Paul and G.E.M. Anscombe (New York: Harper Torchbooks, 1969); Maurice Merleau-Ponty, *The Essential Writings of Merleau-Ponty,* ed. Alden L. Fisher (New York: Harcourt, Brace and World, 1969).

23. James Sellers, *Public Ethics: American Morals and Manners* (New York: Harper & Row, 1970), 40.

24. Albert R. Jonsen and Lewis H. Butler, "Public Ethics and Policy Making," *Hastings Center Report* 5, no. 4 (August 1975): 22.

25. See Peter Medawar, *The Art of the Soluble* (London: Methuen, 1967).

26. See Harold Rosenberg, *Act and the Actor: Making the Self* (New York: New American Library, 1970); Kurt Back, "The Game and the Myth as Two Languages of Social Research," *Behavioral Science* 8 (January 1963): 66–71. For a "mythopoetic" perspective on political actors in the international system, see Paul Ramsey, "A Political Ethics Context for Strategic Thinking," in *Strategic Thinking and Its Moral Implications,* ed. Morton A. Kaplan (Chicago: University of Chicago Center for Policy Study, 1973).

27. Jacques Barzun, *Science, The Glorious Entertainment* (New York: Harper & Row, 1964), 42.

28. See Elizabeth Leonie Simpson, "A Holistic Approach to Moral Development and Behavior," in *Moral Development and Behavior: Theory, Research and Social Issues,* ed. Thomas Lickona (New York: Holt, Rinehart and Winston, 1976), 159–70.

29. See Leo Spitzer, *Linguistics and Literary History: Essays in Stylistics* (Princeton: Princeton University Press, 1948), 19–20, on the principle of the "philological circle," the relation of parts to whole in the hermeneutics of Schleiermacher, Socrates and Plato, and Heidegger; cf. Michael Polanyi, *The Study of Man* (Chicago: University of Chicago Press, 1963), passim.

30. Bernard Williams observes that Socrates's question, "How should one live?," "is not immediate; it is not about what I should do now, or next. It is about a manner of life. The Greeks themselves were much impressed by the idea that such a question must, consequently, be about a whole life and that a good way of living had to issue in what, at its end, would be seen to have been a good life. . . . The idea that one must think, at this very general level, about *a whole life* may seem less compelling to some of us than it did to Socrates. But his question still does press a demand for reflection on one's life *as a whole,* from every aspect and all the way down, even if we do not place as much weight as the Greeks did on how it may end." Quoted in Perry, *Morality, Politics, Law,* 216 n.18.

31. Hannah Arendt, *The Human Condition* (Garden City, N.Y.: Doubleday Anchor, 1959), 4.

32. There are problems with the language of "values." See Robert N. Bellah et al., *Habits of the Heart: Individualism and Commitment in American Life* (Berkeley: University of California, 1985), 80; cf. Ian G. Barbour, "A Definition of Values," in *Technology, Environment, and Human Values* (New York: Praeger, 1980), 60–61.

33. See Marvin E. Frankel, *Partisan Justice* (New York: Hill and Wang, 1980); Jerold S. Auerbach, *Unequal Justice: Lawyers and Social Change in Modern America* (New York: Oxford University Press, 1976). Cf. Kenneth J. Arrow: "A close look reveals that a great deal of economic life depends for its viability on a certain limited degree of ethical commitment. Purely selfish behavior of individuals is really incompatible with any kind of settled economic life." Arrow, "Social Responsibility and Economic Efficiency," *Public Policy,* 1973, 314.

34. See Theodore J. Lowi, *The End of Liberalism: Ideology, Policy, and the Crisis of Public Authority* (New York: Norton, 1969), 41–54.

35. Robert Paul Wolff, *The Poverty of Liberalism* (Boston: Beacon Press, 1969), 131.

36. Quoted in Lowi, *End of Liberalism*, 53.

37. Quoted in Charles P. Loomis and Zona K. Loomis, "Social and Interpersonal Trust—Its Loss by Disjunction," *Humanitas* 9, no. 3 (1973): 325.

38. For an autobiographical account of the development and application of the "principle of complementarity," see Werner Heisenberg, *Physics and Beyond: Encounters and Conversations* (New York: Harper & Row, 1972).

39. For Polanyi's use of the term, see the index to his *Personal Knowledge*.

40. Gladwin Hill, "Nation Set to Observe Earth Day," *New York Times,* 23 April 1970, 36.

41. David Bird, "Earth Day Plans Focus on City," *New York Times,* 20 April 1970, 1.

42. David Bird, "City Announces Earth Day Plan," *New York Times,* 17 April 1970, 51.

43. Gladwin Hill, "Activity Ranges from Oratory to Legislation," *New York Times,* 23 April 1970, 1.

44. Hill, "Nation to Observe Earth Day," 36.

45. Leslie Dunkling, *A Dictionary of Days* (New York: Facts on File, 1988).

46. Amy Sapoworth and Scott Ridley, *The State of the States—1988* (Washington, D.C.: Fund for Renewable Energy and the Environment, Renew America Project, 1989).

47. Council on Environmental Quality, Office of the President, *Environmental Quality,* 17th Annual Report (Washington, D.C.: Government Printing Office, 1986).

48. *State of the States,* 3.

49. Cf. Arendt, *The Human Condition,* 5–6.

Chapter 2. Community, Society, and Ethics

1. See Lynn White, Jr., *Medieval Technology and Social Change* (Oxford: Clarendon Press, 1962); cf. George C. Lodge, *The New American Ideology* (New York: Knopf, 1975), 52–74; Robert Nisbet, *The Quest for Community* (New York: Oxford University Press, 1953), 80.

2. R. H. Tawney, *Religion and the Rise of Capitalism* (New York: New American Library, 1954).

3. Toennies takes the trader and the thinker as symbolic figures in the transition from medieval community to modern society. See Werner J. Cahnman and Rudolf Heberle, eds., *Ferdinand Toennies, On Sociology: Pure, Applied, and Empirical* (Chicago: University of Chicago Press, 1971), 316–32.

4. Will and Ariel Durant, *The Age of Reason Begins* (New York: Simon and Schuster, 1961), 173. The Durants provide a highly readable account of the origins of modern science, as do Jacob Bronowski and Bruce Mazlish in *The Western Intellectual Tradition* (Harmondsworth, England: Penguin, 1963).

5. Raymond Williams, *The Long Revolution* (Harmondsworth, England: Penguin, 1963), 93.

6. Raymond Williams, *Culture and Society, 1780–1950* (Garden City, N.Y.: Doubleday Anchor, 1960), viii.

7. Robert Heilbroner, *The Worldly Philosophers* (New York: Simon and Schuster, 1961), chap. 2, "The Economic Revolution"; Karl Polanyi, *The Great Transformation* (Boston: Beacon Press, 1957), pt. 2, "Rise and Fall of Market Economy."

8. Quoted in Bronowski and Mazlish, *Western Intellectual Tradition,* 422.

9. Polanyi, *Great Transformation,* 141–42.

10. Quoted in Bronowski and Mazlish, *Western Intellectual Tradition,* 500.

11. See "Adam Smith as Sociologist" in Albert Salomon, *In Praise of Enlightenment: Essays in the History of Ideas* (Cleveland: World, 1963), 202–18; Andrew S. Skinner and Thomas Wilson, eds., *Essays on Adam Smith* (Oxford: Clarendon Press, 1975).

12. Jeremy Bentham, *The Principles of Morals and Legislation* (Oxford: Clarendon Press, n.d.), chap. 1, sec. 4.

13. Talcott Parsons, *The Structure of Social Action,* 2d ed. (Glencoe, Ill.: Free Press, 1949), 90.

14. Ibid., 51ff.

15. Quoted in Carl Joachim Friedrich, *The Philosophy of Law in Historical Perspective,* 2d ed. (Chicago: University of Chicago Press, 1963), 97.

16. Quoted in Bronowski and Mazlish, *Western Intellectual Tradition,* 485.

17. See Parsons, *Structure of Social Action,* 89ff.

18. On factual and normative order, see ibid., 89–102; on "natural identity of interests," see 96–97 .

19. See Mary Warnock, *Ethics Since 1900* (London: Oxford University Press, 1966), 1–10; Alasdair MacIntyre, *A Short History of Ethics* (New York: Macmillan, 1966), 244–48.

20. See Jean B. Quandt, *From the Small Town to the Great Community: The Social Thought of Progressive Intellectuals* (New Brunswick: Rutgers University Press, 1970); R. Jackson Wilson, *In Quest of Community: Social Philosophy in the United States, 1860–1920* (New York: Oxford University Press, 1968), 174.

21. See Robert H. Wiebe, *The Search for Order, 1877–1920* (New York: Hill and Wang, 1967), chap. 3; David E. Price, "Community and Control: Critical Democratic Theory in the Progressive Period," *American Political Science Review* 68, no. 4 (December, 1974): 1663–78.

22. Wilson, *In Quest of Community,* 174.

23. See Robert Nisbet, *The Sociological Tradition* (New York: Basic Books, 1966); and Norman Birnbaum's review, "Robert Nisbet's 'The Sociological Tradi-

tion,'" in *Conservative Sociology* (New York: Oxford University Press), 81–93. See also Robert Nisbet, *Tradition and Revolt* (New York: Random House, 1968).

24. Erich Fromm, *Escape from Freedom* (New York: Avon Books, 1965), viii.

25. Max Weber, *The Protestant Ethic and the Spirit of Capitalism*, tr. Talcott Parsons (New York: Scribner's, 1958).

26. Werner Stark, *The Fundamental Forms of Social Thought* (London: Routledge and Kegan Paul, 1962).

27. On these three paradigms, see Larry T. Reynolds and James M. Henslin, eds., *American Society* (New York: McKay, 1971); Norman Birnbaum, *Toward a Critical Sociology* (New York: Oxford University Press, 1971); Alvin Gouldner, *The Coming Crisis of Western Sociology* (New York: Basic Books, 1970); Herman Schwendinger, *The Sociologists of the Chair: A Radical Analysis of the Formative Years of North American Sociology, 1883–1922* (New York: Basic Books, 1974); V.I. Allen, *Social Analysis, A Marxist Critique and Alternative* (London: Longman, 1975); Kenneth M. Dolbeare and Patricia Dolbeare, with Jane Hadley, *American Ideologies,* 2d ed. (Chicago: Rand McNally, 1973).

28. Though it remains very much alive: See Bruce Ackermann, *Social Justice in the Liberal State* (New Haven: Yale University Press, 1980); Richard B. Brandt, "The Real and Alleged Problems of Utilitarianism," *Hastings Center Report* 13, no. 2 (April 1983): 37–43.

29. See Parsons, *Structure of Social Action,* 686ff.; Gunnar Myrdal, *Value in Social Theory,* ed. by Paul Streeten (London: Routledge and Kegan Paul, 1958); Gouldner, *Crisis of Western Sociology,* chap. 3.

30. Michael Polanyi, *Personal Knowledge* (Chicago: University of Chicago Press, 1958), 234; cf. Thomas A. Spragens, Jr., *The Irony of Liberal Reason* (Chicago: University of Chicago Press, 1981).

31. A.I. Melden, "Utility and Moral Reasoning," in *Ethics and Society,* ed. Richard T. DeGeorge (New York: Doubleday, 1966), 173–96.

32. Daniel Bell, *The Coming of Post-Industrial Society* (New York: Basic Books, 1973), 483.

33. Daniel Bell, *The Cultural Contradictions of Capitalism* (New York: Basic Books, 1976).

34. Rudolf Heberle, ed., *Ferdinand Toennies: A New Evaluation* (Chicago: University of Chicago Press, 1971), 109; Cahnman and Heberle, *Toennies, On Sociology,* 91. On the dialectical relation of social concepts, see Paul Diesing, *Patterns of Discovery in the Social Sciences* (Chicago: Aldine-Atherton, 1971), 212–22.

35. See Robert G. Olson, *The Morality of Self-Interest* (New York: Harcourt, Brace and World, 1965).

36. See James Gustafson, "Education for Moral Responsibility," in *Moral Education,* ed. Nancy F. Sizer and Theodore R. Sizer (Cambridge, Mass.: Harvard University Press, 1970), 10–27; Carol Gilligan, *In a Different Voice: Psychological Theory and Women's Development* (Cambridge, Mass.: Harvard University Press, 1982); Craig R. Dykstra, *Vision and Character* (New York: Paulist Press, 1981).

37. Cf. Robert O. Johann, "Love and Justice," in *Ethics and Society,* ed. Richard T. DeGeorge (Garden City, N.Y.: Doubleday Anchor, 1966), esp. 43–44; Knud E. Logstrup, *The Ethical Demand,* tr. Theodor I. Jensen (Philadelphia: Fortress Press, 1971), esp. 23, 119, 130; H.R. Niebuhr, *The Responsible Self: An Essay in Christian Moral Philosophy* (New York: Harper & Row, 1963); John Macmurray, *The Form of the Personal,* vol. 1, *The Self as Agent,* and vol. 2, *Persons in Relation* (London: Faber and Faber, 1957–61).

38. F.H. Heinemann, *Existentialism and the Modern Predicament* (New York: Harper & Brothers, 1958), 192ff.

39. Cf. Paul Tillich, *The Courage to Be* (New Haven: Yale University Press, 1959); Erich Fromm, *The Art of Loving* (New York: Harper Colophon, 1962); Roberto Mangebeira Unger, *Knowledge and Politics* (New York: Free Press, 1975).

40. Morton White, *Toward Reunion in Philosophy* (Cambridge, Mass.: Harvard University Press, 1956), 208–9.

41. See Alasdair MacIntyre, *After Virtue: A Study in Moral Theory* (Notre Dame, Ind.: University of Notre Dame Press, 1981), 63ff.

42. Quoted in Stewart Brand, "Both Sides of the Necessary Paradox," *Harper's,* November 1973, 34.

43. Polanyi, *Personal Knowledge,* 17.

44. Michael Oakeshott, *Rationalism in Politics: And Other Essays* (London: Methuen, 1981), 27.

45. As F.A. Hayek declares, "What new discoveries the federal Constitution contained either resulted from the application of traditional principles to particular problems or emerged as only dimly perceived consequences of general ideas." *The Constitution of Liberty* (Chicago: University of Chicago Press, 1960), 184.

46. Michael Polanyi, *The Tacit Dimension* (Garden City, N.Y.: Doubleday Anchor, 1967), 61–62.

47. Michael Polanyi, *Science, Faith and Society* (London: Oxford University Press, 1946), 56–57.

48. Polanyi, *Personal Knowledge,* 245.

49. MacIntyre, *After Virtue.*

50. Carl J. Friedrich, ed., *The Philosophy of Kant* (New York: Modern Library, 1949), 248.

51. See John Silber, "The Copernican Revolution in Ethics: The Good Reexamined," in Robert Paul Wolff, ed., *Kant* (Garden City, N.Y.: Doubleday Anchor, 1967), 266–90.

52. Hannah Arendt, *The Human Condition* (Garden City, N.Y.: Doubleday Anchor, 1959), 133–39.

53. See Erich Fromm, *The Sane Society* (New York: Holt, Rinehart and Winston, 1960), chap. 5, for features of the capitalistic society that has produced a new social character with a "marketing orientation."

54. Jeremy Bentham, *Constitutional Code,* chap. 12, sec. 6, quoted in Nicholas Rescher, *Distributive Justice* (Indianapolis: Bobbs-Merrill, 1967), 48–49.

55. John Rawls, *The Theory of Justice* (Cambridge, Mass.: Harvard University Press, 1971).

56. Robert Nozick, *Anarchy, State and Utopia* (New York: Basic Books, 1974).

57. Rawls, *Theory of Justice*, chap. 8.

58. Cf. John Thornhill, *The Person and the Group* (Milwaukee: Bruce, 1967), 6; G.H. Sabine, *A History of Political Theory* (London: Harrap, 1948), 131.

59. Thomas Aquinas, *Summa Theologica*, Q.xc.A.2; Aristotle, *Ethics*, V.1; on justice and the polis, Aristotle, *Politics*, bk. I, ch. II, 1253a15. See also Rawls, *Theory of Justice*, 243.

60. At the core of modern liberal jurisprudence is what Unger calls the "antinomy of rules and values": "A system of laws or rules (legal justice) can neither dispense with a consideration of values in the process of adjudication, nor be made consistent with such a consideration. Moreover, judgments about how to further general values in particular situations (substantive justice) can neither do without rules, nor be made compatible with them." Unger, *Knowledge and Politics*, 91.

61. Ibid., 94–99.

62. Cf. Diesing, *Reason in Society*, 125, 142, 168; Huntington Cairns, "The Community as the Legal Order," in *Community*, ed. Carl J. Friedrich (New York: Liberal Arts Press, 1959), 25–49.

63. Richard Taylor, *Good and Evil* (New York: Macmillan, 1970), 138.

64. *Schuringa* v. *City of Chicago* 30 Ill.2d 504, 198 N.E.2d 326 (1964), cited in Dan E. Beauchamp, "Community: The Neglected Tradition of Public Health," *Hastings Center Report* 14, no. 6 (December 1985): 33.

Chapter 3. The Public Realm

1. Alasdair MacIntyre, *After Virtue* (Notre Dame, Ind.: University of Notre Dame Press, 1981), 22.

2. Aristotle, *The Politics*, 1253a28–29, ed. Stephen Everson (New York: Cambridge University Press, 1988), 4.

3. See Hannah Arendt, *The Human Condition* (Garden City, N.Y.: Doubleday, 1959), chap. 5, "Action."

4. Richard Sennett, *The Fall of Public Man* (New York: Knopf, 1977), 3.

5. Ibid., 150ff.

6. Ibid., 221.

7. Ibid., 259.

8. Robert Wiebe, *The Segmented Society: An Introduction to the Meaning of America* (New York: Oxford University Press, 1975), 111.

9. Mason Drukman, *Community and Purpose* (New York: McGraw-Hill, 1971), 399.

10. See Gordon Wood, *The Creation of the American Republic, 1776–1787* (Chapel Hill: University of North Carolina Press, 1969).

11. On changes from 1776 to 1789 and differing interpretations of the Constitution, see Drukman, *Community and Purpose;* Ralph Ketcham, *From Colony to Country: The Revolution in American Thought, 1750–1820* (New York: Macmillan, 1974), 147–48; Bernard Bailyn, *The Ideological Origins of the American Revolution* (Cambridge, Mass.: Harvard University Press, 1967); Garry Wills, *Inventing America: Jefferson's Declaration of Independence* (New York: Vintage Books, 1979). Wills argues strongly against the view that Declaration and Constitution were at odds in any significant way: the signers of the one were the endorsers of the other. There was, however, a discernible shift in the tone of public discourse, as noted by several of the historians cited here.

12. Wood, *Creation of the American Republic,* 55; cf. 61, 608.

13. Ketcham, *From Colony to Country,* 147–48.

14. "Vulgar pragmatism" should not be confused with the philosophical pragmatism associated with Charles Peirce, William James, John Dewey, and others, which represents the distinctive American contribution to philosophy. See John E. Smith, *The Spirit of American Philosophy* (New York: Oxford University Press, 1963).

15. Bailyn, *Ideological Origins of the American Revolution,* 231.

16. Ibid.; see esp. 45, 161.

17. Richard Hofstadter, *The American Political Tradition and the Men Who Made It* (New York: Knopf, 1948), chap. 1; Drukman, *Community and Purpose,* chap. 1.

18. See Grant McConnell, *Private Power and American Democracy* (New York: Vintage Books, 1966), 89ff.

19. See Michael D. Reagan, *The Managed Economy* (New York: Oxford University Press, 1967), chap. 2, "The Jeffersonian Dream Versus Industrial Reality"; John William Ward, "Individualism: Ideology or Utopia?" *Hastings Center Report* 2, no. 3 (September 1974): 17.

20. The phrase is Richard Hofstadter's, in *The American Political Tradition,* chap. 3, "Andrew Jackson and the Rise of Liberal Capitalism."

21. In *L'Ancien régime et la révolution,* cited in Yehoshua Arieli, *Individualism and Nationalism in American Ideology* (Baltimore, Md.: Penguin, 1966), 192–93.

22. Marvin Meyers, *The Jacksonian Persuasion: Politics and Belief* (Stanford: Stanford University Press, 1960), 11.

23. Ibid., 15.

24. Theodore J. Lowi, *The End of Liberalism* (New York: Norton, 1969), pt. 1.

25. See, e.g., Donald J. Devine, *The Political Culture of the United States* (Boston: Little, Brown, 1972), 3 and passim; Sheldon S. Wolin, "Political Theory as a Vocation," *American Political Science Review* 63, no. 4 (December 1969): 1078: the behavioralist's methods of study "presuppose a depth of political culture which his methods of education destroy"; Lane Davis, "The Cost of Realism," in *Apolitical Politics,* ed. Charles A. McCoy and John Playford (New York: Crowell, 1967): "Contemporary democracy is, in fact, a theory dependent on the prior existence of an established community, to the development of which it makes little, if any, contribution" (p. 197).

26. See Henry S. Kariel, ed., *Frontiers of Democratic Theory* (New York: Random House, 1970), pt. 2.

27. John Gardner, "We Have Created the Special Interest State," *Brown University Alumni Magazine,* June 1980, 34.

28. Carl J. Friedrich, "The Concept of Community in the History of Political and Legal Philosophy," in *Community,* ed. Carl J. Friedrich (New York: Liberal Arts Press, 1959), 3.

29. Robert A. Nisbet, *The Sociological Tradition* (New York: Basic Books, 1966), 471.

30. Werner Stark, *The Fundamental Forms of Social Thought* (London: Routledge and Kegan Paul, 1962).

31. Robert Redfield, *The Primitive World and Its Transformations* (Ithaca, N.Y.: Cornell University Press, 1971), 20.

32. Melvin M. Webber, "The Post-City Age," *Daedalus,* Fall 1968, 1099.

33. See Stark, *Fundamental Forms of Social Thought;* Steven Lukes, *Individualism* (New York: Harper Torchbook, 1973).

34. Quoted in Lukes, *Individualism,* 151.

35. Robert N. Bellah, Richard Madsen, William M. Sullivan, Ann Swidler, and Steven M. Tipton, *Habits of the Heart: Individualism and Commitment in American Life* (Berkeley: University of California Press, 1985).

36. E.g., review atricles by John F. Wilson and Barbara Hargrove in *Religious Studies Review* 14, no. 4 (October 1988): 304–9, and "Symposium: Habits of the Heart" in *Soundings* 69, nos. 1–2 (Spring/Summer 1968), esp. Jeffrey Stout, "Liberal Society and the Languages of Morals," 32–59. Stout differs with Bellah and with Alasdair MacIntyre on the lack of common moral ground in American society; see his *Ethics after Babel* (Boston: Beacon Press, 1988).

37. Fredric Jameson, "On *Habits of the Heart*," *South Atlantic Quarterly* 86, no. 4 (Fall 1987): 545–65.

38. Bellah et al., *Habits of the Heart,* 127; cf. Jameson, "On *Habits*," 562.

39. Sennett, *Fall of Public Man,* 259.

40. Quoted in Craig Calhoun, "Populist Politics, Communications Media and Large Scale Societal Integration," *Sociological Theory* 6 (Fall 1988): 225.

41. Ibid., 226.

42. Ibid.; Jürgen Habermas, *The Theory of Communicative Action,* vol. 1, *Reason and the Rationalization of Society,* trans. T. McCarthy (Boston: Beacon Press, 1984); vol. 2, *System and Lifeworld,* trans. T. McCarthy (Boston: Beacon Press, 1987); T. McCarthy, *The Critical Theory of Jürgen Habermas* (Cambridge, Mass.: MIT Press, 1978).

43. Calhoun, "Populist Politics," 224.

44. Ibid., 227ff.

45. Ronald Steele, *Walter Lippmann and the American Century* (Boston: Little, Brown, 1980), 496.

46. Quoted in Philip Gold, *Advertising, Politics, and American Culture: From Salesmanship to Therapy* (New York: Paragon House, 1987), 150.

47. Ralph Hummel, *The Bureaucratic Experience,* 3d ed. (New York: St. Martin's Press, 1987), 180. This and the preceding paragraph draw on Hummel.

48. Wendell Berry, *Standing by Words* (San Francisco: North Point Press, 1983), 38.

49. Ibid., 39.

50. Wendell Berry, *Home Economics* (San Francisco: North Point Press, 1987), 48–53.

51. Quoted in Studs Terkel, *The Great Divide* (New York: Pantheon, 1988), 359.

52. Elizabeth Janeway, *Powers of the Weak* (New York: Knopf, 1980), 315.

53. Kai T. Erikson, *Everything in Its Path: Destruction of Community in the Buffalo Creek Flood* (New York: Simon and Schuster, 1976), 186–245.

54. Ibid., 258.

55. Robert Reich, "Policy Making in a Democracy," in *The Power of Public Ideas* (Cambridge, Mass.: Ballinger, 1988), 123–56.

56. Ibid., 142.

57. National Assessment of Educational Progress, *Crossroads in American Education,* cited in *Time,* 27 February 1989, 68.

Chapter 4. Choosing Who We Are

1. Donald J. Devine, *The Political Culture of the United States* (Boston: Little, Brown, 1972), 3–4. For a discussion of core values in the American civic culture, see Kenneth L. Karst, *Belonging to America: Equal Citizenship and the Constitution* (New Haven and London: Yale University Press, 1989).

2. Louis Hartz, *The Liberal Tradition in America: An Interpretation of American Political Thought Since the Revolution* (New York: Harcourt, Brace and World, 1955).

3. Ralph Barton Perry, *Puritanism and Democracy* (New York: Harper Torchbooks, 1964): "The separation of church and state, the diversity of religious creeds freely held and lived within a common civil framework, the spirit of inquiry and discussion, the ideal of voluntary agreement, the appeal from the political authority to the universal human faculties of conscience and reason, the sentiments of equality and humanity—all these were all cherished within the bosom of Puritanism against the time when their fuller implications could be realized in appropriate political and legal institutions" (p. 359). See Michael McGiffert, ed., *Puritanism and the American Experience* (Reading, Mass.: Addison-Wesley, 1969).

4. Devine, *Political Culture of the United States,* chap. 4, esp. 182–230.

5. Alexis de Tocqueville, *Democracy in America,* ed. Richard D. Heffner (New York: New American Library, 1956), 195.

6. David Potter, *People of Plenty* (Chicago: University of Chicago Press, 1954);

see also David Noble on the myth of the frontier in historiography, in *Historians Against History* (St. Paul: University of Minnesota Press, 1967).

7. Perry Miller, "The Protestant Ethic," in McGiffert, *Puritanism*, 128–29.

8. See Fernand Braudel, *Capitalism and Material Life, 1400–1800*, tr. Miriam Kochan (New York: Harper & Row, 1973).

9. See Richard Hofstadter, *Social Darwinism in American Thought, 1860–1915* (Philadelphia: University of Pennsylvania Press, 1944).

10. See Yehoshua Arieli, *Individualism and Nationalism in American Ideology* (Baltimore, Md.: Penguin, 1966), 341–42.

11. Ibid., 326–27.

12. Garry B. Nash, *Red, White, and Black* (Englewood Cliffs, N.J.: Prentice-Hall, 1974), xiv.

13. Michael Kammen, *Sovereignty and Liberty: Constitutional Discourse in American Culture* (Madison: University of Wisconsin Press, 1988), 56; on "liberty," see Robert H. Webking, *The American Revolution and the Politics of Liberty* (Baton Rouge: Louisiana State University Press, 1988).

14. Isaiah Berlin, "Two Concepts of Liberty," in *Four Essays on Liberty* (London: Oxford University Press, 1969), esp. 121–22.

15. C.B. Macpherson, *Democratic Theory: Essays in Retrieval* (London: Oxford University Press, 1973), 116.

16. See Mortimer J. Adler, *We Hold These Truths: Understanding the Ideas and Ideals of the Constitution* (New York: Macmillan, 1987), pt. 4, "The Emergent Ideal of Democracy."

17. Ibid., 215.

18. John E. Ferling, *The First of Men: A Life of George Washington* (Knoxville: University of Tennessee Press, 1988), 475.

19. Stanley M. Elkins, *Slavery: A Problem in American Institutional and Intellectual Life* (Chicago: University of Chicago Press, 1959), 37ff.

20. Ibid., 51ff.

21. E.L. Doctorow, "A Citizen Reads the Constitution," in *America in Theory*, ed. Leslie Berlowitz, Denis Donoghue, Louis Menand (London: Oxford University Press, 1988), 296.

22. See Alvin Toffler, *Future Shock* (New York: Bantam Books, 1971), 303–4; Devine, *Political Culture of the United States*, 291ff.; Seymour Martin Lipset, *The First New Nation* (New York: Basic Books, 1963); Geoffery Gorer, *The American People: A Study in National Character* (New York: Norton, 1948); Robert Lynd, *Knowledge for What?* (New York: Grove Press, 1964; orig. publ. 1939); Philip Slater, *The Pursuit of Loneliness* (Boston: Beacon Press, 1971).

23. See Karen Horney, *The Neurotic Personality of Our Time* (New York: Norton, 1937); Hendrik M. Ruitenbeek, *The Individual and the Crowd: A Study of Identity in America* (New York: New American Library, 1964); Wilson Carey McWilliams, *The Idea of Fraternity in America* (Berkeley: University of California Press, 1973), 107, 109.

24. Daniel Bell, *The Coming of Post-Industrial Society* (New York: Basic Books, 1973), 480; see 475–89, "Culture and Consciousness."

25. This description is drawn from Donald T. Campbell's presidential address to the American Psychological Association in 1975, reprinted from *American Psychologist* 30 (1975) in *Zygon* 11, no. 3 (September 1976): 167–208. See also Peter Marin, "The New Narcissism," *Harper's,* October 1975, 45–56; Christopher Lasch, *The Culture of Narcissism: American Life in an Age of Diminishing Expectations* (New York: Norton, 1978); Barry Schwartz, *The Battle for Human Nature: Science, Morality and Modern Life* (New York: London, 1986). See Michael A. Wallach and Lisa Wallach, *Psychology's Sanction for Selfishness: The Error of Egoism in Theory and Therapy* (San Francisco: Freeman, 1983), for a trenchant criticism of egoistic psychology and a constructive alternative view.

26. Campbell, address, 197.

27. Ibid., 198.

28. See Barry Schwartz, *The Battle for Human Nature* (New York: Norton, 1986); Amitai Etzioni, *The Moral Dimension: Toward a New Economics* (New York: Free Press, 1988). The phrase "unencumbered self" is from Michael Sandel, *Liberalism and the Limits of Justice* (New York: Cambridge University Press, 1982).

29. Richard Musgrave, *The Theory of Public Finance* (New York: McGraw-Hill, 1959), 10; Bruce R. Bolnick, "Collective Goods Provision through Community Development," *Economic Development and Cultural Change* 25, no. 1 (October 1976): 138.

30. Gordon Allport, *Personality and Social Encounter* (Boston: Beacon Press, 1964), 202.

31. Erik Erikson, *Identity, Youth and Crisis* (New York: Norton, 1968), 260; cf. Robert V. Hannaford, "Patterns in the Growth of Meaning Drawn from the Behavioral Sciences," *Ethics* 74, no. 1 (October 1963): 53–60. See also Pitirim A. Sorokin, *Altruistic Love* (Boston: Beacon Press, 1950).

32. Quoted in Steven Lukes, *Individualism* (New York: Harper Torchbooks, 1973), 151.

33. Erik Erikson, *Insight and Responsibility* (New York: Norton, 1964), 155–56; see also 233.

34. See William Ryan, *Blaming the Victim* (New York: Vintage Books, 1971).

35. Devine, *Political Culture of the United States,* 260–65.

36. Lester C. Thurow, *The Zero-Sum Solution: Building a World-Class American Economy* (New York: Simon and Schuster), 120.

37. The following books propose specific policies to this end: Martin Carnoy and Derek Shearer, *Economic Democracy: The Challenge of the 1980's* (Armonk, N.Y.: M.E. Sharpe, 1980); Paul G. King and David O. Woodyard, *The Journey toward Freedom: Economic Structures and Theological Perspectives* (London: Associated University Presses, 1982); Mark A. Lutz and Kenneth Lux, *The Challenge of Humanistic Economics* (London: Benjamin Cummings Publishing, 1979).

38. *Economic Justice for All: Pastoral Letter on Catholic Social Teaching and the U.S.*

Economy (Washington, D.C.: U.S. Catholic Conference, 1986), 15. First sentence, italicized in the original, is taken from *Mater et Magistra,* 219–20. See *Pastoral Constitution,* 63.

39. See Leonard Silk, "Bishops' Letter and U.S. Goals," *New York Times,* 14 November 1984, D2.

40. "Second Draft of the U.S. Bishops' Pastoral Letter on Catholic Social Teaching and the U.S. Economy," *Origins* (NC Documentary Service) 15, no. 17 (10 October 1985): 257–96; James E. Hug, *Renew the Earth: A Guide to the Second Draft of the U.S. Bishops' Pastoral Letter on Catholic Social Teaching and the U.S. Economy* (Washington, D.C.: Center of Concern, n.d.).

41. Ibid., 131.

42. Hug, *Renew the Earth,* 25.

43. *Economic Justice for All,* p. 261, sec. 33.

44. Ibid., p. 260, sec. 20.

45. Ibid., p. 268, sec. 96.

46. The account that follows is based on Frye Gaillard, *The Dream Long Deferred* (Chapel Hill: University of North Carolina Press, 1988).

47. Ibid., 52.

48. Ibid., 146.

49. Ibid., 147.

50. Ibid., xv.

51. Ibid., 182.

52. *News and Observer,* 18 April 1989.

Chapter 5. Starting from Here

1. Søren Kierkegaard, *The Present Age,* trans. Alexander Dru (New York: Harper & Row, 1962), 60.

2. Ibid., 79.

3. Quoted in Kathleen Hall Jamieson, *Eloquence in an Electronic Age* (New York: Oxford University Press, 1988), 60.

4. Ibid., 61.

5. Paul Tillich, *Systematic Philosophy,* vol. 1 (Chicago: University of Chicago Press, 1955), 239; cf. Susanne Langer, *Philosophy in a New Key* (New York: Mentor Books, 1955), 42–63.

6. *Time,* 19 September 1988, 100.

7. Philip Slater, *The Pursuit of Loneliness* (Boston: Beacon Press, 1970), 15.

8. Michael Harrington, *The Other America: Poverty in the United States* (Baltimore, Md.: Penguin Books, 1963).

9. Hannah Arendt, *The Human Condition* (Garden City, N.Y.: Doubleday Anchor, 1959), 219.

10. Quoted in Neil Postman, *Amusing Ourselves to Death: Public Discourse in the Age of Show Business* (New York: Viking Penguin, 1985), 125.

11. Ibid., 126, 129–37.

12. Quoted in James F. Lea, *Political Consciousness and American Democracy* (Jackson: University Press of Mississippi, 1982), 57.

13. Daniel J. Boorstin, *The Americans: The Democratic Experience* (New York: Random House, 1973). Boorstin's paean of praise to the commercial republic is reflected in his introduction to pt. 2: "Never before had so many men been united by so many things" (p. 90). And later: "Did the human richness of American democracy come not from the attainment of wealth, but from the reaching for it? . . . Perhaps the best things in democracy came not from having but from seeking, not from being well off but from becoming better off" (p. 390).

14. Quoted in Michael Paul Rogin, *Ronald Reagan, the Movie* (Berkeley: University of California Press, 1988), 3.

15. The authors, James Stout and Frederick Rivara, pediatricians, reviewed five earlier studies in an article in the journal *Pediatrics,* as reported in the *Durham Morning Herald,* 31 March 1989, 5.

16. Wendell Berry, *The Hidden Wound* (Boston: Houghton Mifflin, 1970).

17. Ibid., 88.

18. Ibid., 83.

19. Ibid., 144–45.

20. Anastasia Toufexis, "Now for a Woman's Point of View," *Time,* 17 April 1989, 52.

21. Jean Bethke Elshtain, "Afterwords," in *Human Nature and Public Policy,* ed. Lynette Friedrich-Cofer (New York: Praeger, 1986), 324.

22. Mortimer J. Adler, *We Hold These Truths* (New York: Macmillan, 1987), 56. Cf. Michael J. Perry, *Morality, Politics, and Law* (New York: Oxford University Press, 1988), chaps. 1 and 2. Thomas Jefferson's own view of happiness has to be understood as scientific, moral, and political, against the background of the Scottish Enlightenment, according to Garry Wills. The phrase "pursuit of happiness" referred to public happiness in which the individual would find happiness. See *Inventing America: Jefferson's Declaration of Independence* (New York: Vintage Books, 1979), 313 and chaps. 10, 17, 18.

23. Ellen Goodman, "Hot Tubs, Microwaves, VCR Nice, but They're Not the American Dream," *Durham Morning Herald,* 16 May 1989, 5A.

24. Joshua Wiener, quoted in Charles Green, "Congress Wary of Long-Term Health Care," *Durham Morning Herald,* 18 May 1989, 1.

25. Harry R. Moody, *Abundance of Life: Human Development Policies for an Aging Society* (New York: Columbia University Press, 1988), 25.

26. *Setting Limits,* 21.

27. Moody, *Abundance of Life,* 24–26.

28. Ibid., 4–8.

29. Ibid., 90–91.

30. Ibid., 190–99; on notion of the "three boxes of life," see 28.

31. Ibid., 120.

32. See Fritjof Capra, *The Turning Point: Science, Society, and the Rising Culture* (New York: Simon and Schuster, 1982), esp. chap. 2, "The Newtonian World-Machine."

33. Quoted in Laurence Foss and Kenneth Rothenberg, *The Second Medical Revolution: From Biomedicine to Infomedicine* (Boston: New Science Library, 1987), 7.

34. Ibid., 234–35.

35. Leonard A. Sagan, *The Health of Nations: True Causes of Sickness and Well-Being* (New York: Basic Books, 1987), 195.

36. Quoted in ibid., 194.

37. Ibid., 199.

38. Andrew H. Malcolm, "New Efforts Developing Against the Hate Crime," *New York Times,* 12 May 1989, A12.

39. Sagan, *Health of Nations,* 182–83.

40. Ibid., 183.

41. *New York Times,* 18 May 1989, A7.

42. *Ratchford* v. *Gay Lib* 434 U.S. 1080, 1082 reh'g denied, 435 U.S. 981 (1978). Quoted in Dan E. Beauchamp, *The Health of the Republic: Epidemics, Medicine, and Moralism as Challenges to Democracy* (Philadelphia: Temple University Press, 1988), 208.

43. Martin Marty, *The Public Church: Mainline-Evangelical-Catholic* (New York: Crossroad, 1981), 3.

44. Quoted in Alan Geyer, *Piety and Politics: American Protestantism in the World Arena* (Richmond, Va.: John Knox Press, 1963), 31–32.

45. Daniel Bell, *The Cultural Contradictions of Capitalism* (New York: Basic Books, 1976), 245.

46. *1985 Annual Report,* General Board of Church and Society, United Methodist Church, Washington, D.C.

47. See the *Hastings Center Report,* published bimonthly by The Hastings Center, 255 Elm Road, Briarcliff Manor, NY.

48. *President's Commission for the Study of Ethical Problems in Medicine and Behavioral Research* (Washington, D.C.: The Commission, 1982).

INDEX